Kitchen Shortcuts:
Saving Time & Money
In the Minutes You Have

Marie Swedberg

Kitchen Shortcuts:
Saving Time & Money
In the Minutes You Have

Marnie Swedberg

The Marnie Method Series for Super Busy Women
Visit http://www.Marnie.com

Book III. **The Marnie Method**
Series for Super Busy Women.

Kitchen Shortcuts:
Saving Time & Money
In the Minutes You Have

Copyright 2011
by **Marnie Swedberg**
http://www.Marnie.com

Cover Design by
Paul Teleron

Layout Design by
Surendra Gupta

Cover Quotes from

Rebecca Lisell

For more information contact:
Gifts of Encouragement, Inc.
2360 Corporate Circle, Suite 400
Henderson, NV 89014
877-77-HOW-TO
Info@Marnie.com
http://www.Marnie.com.

Swedberg, Marnie.
    Kitchen Shortcuts: Saving Time & Money in the Minutes You Have/by Marnie Swedberg
            p.   cm.

ISBN 0-98299-352-1
1. Cooking.   2. Cooking Methods: Professional.   3. Cooking: Reference.   1. Kitchen Shortcuts

First Edition/Book: 2011

Table of Contents

Acknowledgements

Thanks to my family, #1 fans, and faithful taste testers:

Dave, Mark, Keren and Tim, plus the thousands of guests I've had the honor to serve in our home, at parties and events I've hosted or catered, at M&K Takeouts, and at Soulutions Over Coffee Espresso Café.

Thanks to the book contributors:

Lynnette Danielson, Michael Danielson, Karen Fausher, Nancy Fisher, Vicki Foster, Marla Hartson, Linda Hecker, Susan Helweg, Evie Mehlhaff, Marcia Mehlhaff, Kendra Nash, Doris Swedberg, Jessie Weaver.

Thanks also to my publishing team from around the world:

Cenon Gaytos, Dyann Alon, Jill Schrupp, Kari Anderson, Kassandra K., Mariella Mojar, Kel Santiago, Paul Teleron Romela Moncatar, Surendra Gupta.

Thanks to my staffs at M&K, Soulutions and Gifts, Inc. You have covered my back for months on end as we've prepared this book for republication. Never could have done it without you!

M&K Takeouts. Isaac Anderson, Penny Anderson, Danae Clark, Julia Fisher, Winter Johnson, Joel Maxwell, Ryan

Maxwell, Seth Maxwell, Hannah Moyer, Mattea Oatman, Theresa Oatman, Rosie Orvis, Kim Ramiller, Natalie Ramiller, Shelbi Rassier, Alexander Richert, Jeremy Thompson.

Soulutions & Over Coffee. Nicol Eichenberger, Deidre Hahn, Joanna Heppner, Karen Holmberg-Smith, Lissa Holmberg-Smith, Susie Lucca, Michelle Maxwell, Lacey Milbrath, Natalie Ramiller, Rylie Scharfenkamp, Laurie Thompson.

Gifts of Encouragement, Inc. Kevin Campbell, Danae Clark, Katie Deal, Donte Dinish, Surendra Gupta, Lotfi Messaoudi, Nancy Peterson, MC Ramon, Michele Reynolds, Jonas Tandinco, Paul Teleron, Chris Wright.

Thanks to every mom, home economics teacher, adult education provider and college professor who has used this book in part or its entirety to train current or future home food managers.

Thanks to every librarian who has assisted me. Special thanks to the director, Barbara Jauquet-Kalinoski, staff and librarians of the Northwest Regional Libraries, who provided encouragement and support as I coordinated over 100 events for them while publishing this book.

Finally, thanks to all of you who support me in any way. The list is too long to include here, but please know that I consider myself blessed beyond measure for your participation in my life.

Marnie's Prayer for You

May your family mealtimes be fun,
the laughter around your table contagious,
and your every kitchen encounter enjoyable.

May your children be healthy and kind,
learning beside you to cook fast and smart,
as together you make and share meals with many.

May your budget be robust,
your free time plenteous,
and your future bright.

Introduction

B.U.S.Y.

Best Unique Strategies for You!

This book is for you if you need to get dinner on the table for your family, teach a class on cooking, manage your restaurant more efficiently or host a large party for fun or function.

Regardless of whether you are serving dinner to your own family or sharing a feast with friends, the re-release of Kitchen Shortcuts offers an essential tool to help you get control of your food budget, spend less time in the kitchen, and provide delicious and healthy food for family and friends.

- It can be read, cover-to-cover, in less than two hours.
- It offers hundreds of simple, practical, doable hints and how-tos on every aspect of kitchen management.
- It lays a structured foundation of smart strategies, which serve as a launching pad for your creative ideas.
- Once you master the concepts, you'll be able to apply them to every recipe you love.
- It is simple, but it's not intuitive.

Most cooks apply one or more of the strategies, and find success. Readers of Kitchen Shortcuts who apply multiple strategies simultaneously enjoy remarkable outcomes.

When I wrote this book the first time, I did so after interlibrary-loaning over 100 how-to books, seeking the one that explained what it was I was doing. People were asking me how I was doing my food (fast, tasted great, cost less, and so on), and I was determined to just find the book that explained it so I could tell them to read that.

When I couldn't find one, I interlibrary-loaned a bunch of books on how to write a book. It took me two years to complete the manuscript and an additional 18 months for it be published by St. Martin's Press, a big New York City publishing house.

Now, 15 years later, you can find most of my strategies online and in other books. What you can't find anywhere else but here is the entire strategic system, in one coherent, easy-to-read book.

The strategies in the book have revolutionized many home- and professional- kitchens. I've received letters from home economics teachers, restaurant owners, and others who have used the strategies with great success. I've received phone calls from all across America from people who found real time and money savings after reading the book. One reader explained, through tears, how the book had saved her husband's life. His health had been deteriorating for months, but after switching to the homemade dry mixes and home cooked meals, he began to get better. In the end, they found that he was allergic to additives found in most packet mixes.

When the first edition of the book was released in 1996, I was routinely entertaining more than 100 guests a month in our home. Now, because we own a restaurant, we routinely entertain more than 100 guests a day.

The revised version of Kitchen Shortcuts includes the best of the original material, some additional shortcuts I've discovered in the interim, and my entire proven system to help you save time and money while pulling off great-tasting meals that the whole family and guests will enjoy.

Chapter 1

Money Saving Strategies

This is the book for people who need to
save time without spending extra money, but who
also need to save money without spending extra time.

How would you feel toward a friend who gifted you with 48 hours of free time plus an envelope full of hundred dollar bills? Kitchen Shortcuts has that effect on busy home food managers. Marla Hartson, a mom and engineering consultant says, "To a homemaker, this book might make the difference between spending lots or less time cooking. To me it makes the difference between ordering a pizza or serving a home-cooked meal."

USDA.gov reports that the average family spends half their grocery budget in restaurants. This costs families two to five times the equivalent servings at home: restaurants have to charge to cover the cost of the building, equipment, licenses, advertising, insurance, taxes, employees, and more.

In this chapter we'll explore effective money-saving strategies to help you drive by the drive-thrus to enjoy a healthy homemade meal in the minutes you have. You'll learn how to make a personalized, flexible, and bullet-proof menu plan, organize your kitchen for speed and efficiency, shop smart, and much more.

Eating Out

Despite the extra cost, all of us have reasons and certain seasons that justify the expense of eating out. Some of mine include eating out while traveling, going out to celebrate an achievement, birthday or anniversary, satisfying a craving for a certain taste I can't make at home, and sitting to be served instead of doing the work myself.

All of these reasons are legitimate, but not necessarily the only way to go about it.

- When traveling alone or with limited time, I usually choose a buffet. With only three exceptions nationwide in ten years of testing, I have always been allowed to request a take-out box which is billed by the pound instead of at the going buffet rate. By taking my average serving size (instead of too much, a common buffet complaint), I typically pay $2-$4 and walk out in less than five minutes with a balanced meal featuring fruit, salad, entrée, sides, and a bite-sized dessert.
- When traveling for pleasure, a quick stop online or in person to the tourist center provides astounding discount coupons from local restaurants.
- When you are hungry for a certain taste, there are sites online like CopyCat.com which specialize in offering look-alike recipes from your favorite restaurants. Trying new recipes like this can serve as your weekend entertainment. Invite friends to "taste-test" your results.
- Being served is one of my favorite reasons for eating out that can also be accomplished at home. My husband and kids have sometimes prepared a meal, served it family style and cleaned it all up. It worked. It gave me the break I needed while creating great memories for all of us.
- When planning a special occasion, restaurants may be the best place, but don't rule out hosting at least some of the party at home, even just dessert. This book will give you great options for pulling off pain-free parties quick and for a fraction of a group dining tab.

I honestly love going out to eat! But I do it for pleasure, which, according to FastFood-Statistics.blogspot.com, is not the norm. Their statistics show that over 50 million people in the United States depend on fast food for their sustenance. They either don't know how to cook at home, don't think they have time to make home cooked meals, don't comprehend how much money they are wasting on fast food, or don't grasp how much healthier it can be to eat at home.

By using the shortcuts in this book, you will be able to dine at home, on foods you love, and save money every time you do.

Saving money pays. If you invest $25 per week in the stock market, at 12% annual interest, for 20 years, you will have $100,000. After 30 years, you'll have $300,000.

Prioritizing Family Meals

The biggest reason to eat at home isn't necessarily the money, although that is a big motivation.

National Merit Society studies prove that shared family mealtimes lead to high-achieving kids and to increased stability in marriage and improvements in work performance.

When our own children were small, my goal was to enjoy structured mealtimes every day. As they hit the teen years with all the sports and jobs, and with the purchase of our family businesses, my goal became to host structured mealtimes whenever it was possible.

Whatever your goals, knowing how to save time on food prep can make the difference between serving a family meal and punting with fast food or other more expensive options. The strategies in this book allow you to:

- eat at home anytime you want, regardless of how busy you are.
- avoid wasting time on midweek trips to the grocery store, picking up missing meal components.
- enjoy savings of up to 80% by using small snatches of time to make your own dry mixes.

- know that your freezer is full of homemade convenience options that you made with time you were going to spend in the kitchen anyway.

As you implement the how-to's in this book, you'll find yourself spending less money on food and less time in the kitchen. You will realize immediate savings by making even a few small changes. Best of all, you'll have the joy of serving your family healthy, homemade meals whenever you want.

The purpose of sharing my kitchen secrets is to help you better manage your food-spending instead of letting it manage you. Taking control means finding and stopping the time- and money-leaks.

This book will highlight potential trouble spots in your current routine and provide strategies for repairing or eliminating them. We'll focus on:

- quick fixes. Did you know that by cutting out just one midweek trip to the grocery store you can save up to an hour in travel, parking, shopping and storage time, and as much as $100 on the food itself?
- organizational strategies. You will learn to organize your pantry and kitchen for efficiency.
- long-term solutions. You'll gain the skills needed to serve great meals with or without advance notice using the ingredients you have on hand.
- effective prioritization of your food, time, and nutritional goals.

Each of our lives, households, and families is unique, but it seems universal that we'd all like more time and more money to pursue our dreams. Great gains can be made in these areas as we learn to manage the home kitchen.

Money-Saving Impromptu Meals

Opportunities to drive thru and lose are on every corner. When you are tired and hungry, the only thing that will keep you on the straight and narrow is the assurance that something easy and appealing awaits you at home. At moments like these, the realization that you are paying upwards of thirty dollars an hour for someone else to assemble your subs, salads, burgers or fries is only slightly convincing. Having a workable menu plan will usually make the difference between spending and saving.

After a number of years of experimenting with highly structured menu plans, I settled contentedly into a relaxed approach for deciding what to make. The first step to success was creating notebooks containing my all-time favorite recipes.

I now simply grab my notebook full of "Main Dishes," sometimes as late as fifteen minutes before a meal is served, and choose something that sounds good. The impromptu plan works because I have a stocked pantry with all the ingredients I need to make anything in my recipe repertoire. (I'll explain more about how to do this in a few pages.)

Someday I may have a computer in my kitchen, but I might always prefer a paper-recipe over even a laptop… not sure yet! Anyway, at least for now, I've clipped and taped all my favorite recipes, from their original sources, into one of these 3-ring binders. Binder title panels read: Main Dishes, Soups, Salads & Sides, Breakfasts & Breads, and Desserts.

The binders allow me to find any recipe I own in seconds, and combined with the strategies I share in the upcoming pages, including the master shopping list and stocked pantry, they allow me to make anything I want in minutes. The freedom to be this flexible allows me to cook great meals no matter how busy or stressful the day.

Menu Planning for Additional Time & Money Savings

Michael E. Gerber, the author of *E-Myth*, teaches restaurant owners to succeed by helping them think like a franchise. You will enjoy noticeable money and time savings in your home kitchen as soon as you begin to think like a restaurateur.

Imagine walking into a Chick-fil-A® and ordering Filet Mignon and a spinach salad. They would just smile, and maybe even feel sort of sorry for you, because your choice is not on the menu. Their kitchen is not prepared to serve that meal.

It's the same at home. Think back to the last time you walked into your own kitchen, wanting to cook a certain meal, but didn't have the right ingredients. Maybe you felt a bit sorry for yourself.

Unlike the majority of kitchens, restaurants don't run out of food unless: a) there is some type of crises in the world, b) there is poor management, or c) they are using a scarcity technique to drive daily specials (often to use up extras).

Thinking like a restaurateur, at least in this particular angle of things, will streamline every minute you spend in the kitchen.

The first thing to do is to come up with at least seven key recipes, one for each day of the week. These should be your favorite, quick-to-fix meals. Ideally, you will want to make a thirty-day meal rotation plan (see the sample on page 9), but start with at least seven.

You may list only entrées or both main and side dishes. Feel free to choose all unique meals or to include a few repetitive meals. Your menu plan will be as unique as if you were opening your own restaurant. The key to success is to find the fast and fabulous combinations that will keep you cooking, even on the busiest days.

The menu plan is great because it is flexible while providing just enough structure to keep you on track.

Plan to use your leftovers efficiently. For example, from time to time I make a Thanksgiving-size turkey or large turkey breast. Occasionally I make stuffing (recipe on page 74) and use the extras for Layered Turkey Bake (page 51), but more often I just bake potatoes.

Sample Menu Rotation Plan

Sunday	Monday	Tuesday	Weds	Thursday	Friday	Saturday
Roast	Turkey Rice Pilaf	Chicken in a Jiffy	Yorkshire Strata	Pan Fried Fish	Parmigiano	Steak with Grill Sauce
Roast	Alfredo Chicken	Turkey Meatballs Tetrazzini	Spaghetti	Stir-Fry	Layered Turkey Bake	Swiss Steak
Roast	Turkey	Beef Stew	Glazed Chicken Breast	Meatballs Consommé	Tamale Pie	Creamed Steak Filets
Roast	BBQ Meatballs	Stir-Fry	Layered Tamale Pie	Lasagna	Burritos	Chicken Fried Steak
Roast	Glazed Ham & Potatoes	Spaghetti Pie	Chow Mein	Turkey Salsa Quickies	Grilled Chicken Breast	Steak with Grill Sauce

I always make gravy and use the leftover pan juices for stew. You could pay several dollars per pound for deli turkey or you could buy large birds for a fraction of that cost and save the difference quite easily by thinly slicing your extra meat and freezing it in meal-size portions.

If your family insists on the "see whole turkey, eat whole turkey" mentality, consider cooking your bird overnight at 250°F. This gives you the opportunity to take care of the turkey in the morning, after it has cooked and cooled, when your family will not be so tempted to devour a Thanksgiving-size meal. You may be able to stash all the meat before they even know you've cooked a bird.

The amount of turkey meat required in a casserole dinner for four is equal to only a pound or so of meat, while the amount you consume when you serve turkey as the main course is closer to a pound per person, so it pays to serve combo dishes instead of always straight meat with sides.

Once you have written out your menu plan, post one in your kitchen where hungry family members can find an answer to the familiar question, "What's for supper?"

If the scheduled meal for the day can't work, for whatever reasons, simply replace it with another easy-to-assemble or previously expanded freezer meal. You're in charge; you can do this.

Plans and schedules should never box you in. They should support your needs. The goal of a menu plan is freedom and flexibility.

Once you know what you want to serve your family, the next logical step is to shop for the ingredients.

The Master Shopping List

How many times during the past month have you had to stop by the supermarket for a missing dinner component or other needed items? Alternatively, how many times have you ruled out a meal idea because you didn't have the necessary ingredients?

Living without a functional grocery shopping list is like reinstalling your computer operating system and programs prior to every use. You would never do that.

Yet, most home cooks use a scratch pad or no list at all and assume they'll make wise financial choices in stores laid out by marketing geniuses. In addition, according to Food Marketing Institute (www.FMI.org), each store features somewhere around 50,000 items from which you must choose. Walking in without a plan is like walking into a brick wall – it's going to hurt.

I can tell you, for a time, this was my habit, and it was a major drain on my schedule and food budget. Gopher trips to the supermarket cost extra in every way—gas, money for impulse items, and time spent driving, standing in line, and handling the purchases once home.

The simple act of creating a Master Shopping List and posting it in your kitchen eliminates all this wasted time, effort, and expense, and enables you to meet all your grocery needs in just one trip per week.

Follow these seven steps to go from zero to hero in the least time possible.

Step 1. Decide on a grocery list format.

- I have posted my own editable Word.doc at www.Marnie.com for you. Just visit the FREE STUFF page. If you know how to use text boxes in Microsoft Word, this one is easy to tweak and use.
- Search the web for your favorite grocery store. Look on their site for their online shopping list. Some of these shopping lists are remarkably editable and user friendly while some are less so.
- Use or look for sites like www.aislebyaisle.com. At the time of this writing, this site includes instructions on how to make grocery lists with your own items and lay them out in the order of your store, plus lots more bells and whistles for a small monthly fee.

Step 2. Print out one rough draft of your list.

Step 3. Personalize it by identifying which items to include on your list.

- Include everything needed to make the seven (or more) meals on your rotating menu plan, plus other items you regularly use.
- Most lists consist of about 200 items total, so while it sounds daunting, it's really not that bad.
- It's easiest if you flip through your recipe cards and books, and peek inside your cupboards, refrigerator, and freezer to refresh your memory.
- Once you have your inventory list typed up, organize the items by category: dairy foods, frozen foods, produce, baking supplies, paper products, cereals, and so on. By grouping similar items, you'll save time in the store by making one trip around, and one trip only. No more backtracking through the supermarket aisles for missing items.

Step 4. Make and save your changes. Print out one trial list.

Step 5. Post your new shopping list in plain view in your kitchen and ask your family members to help keep it current. As your week proceeds, highlight items as you think of them or as you use them up. Your grocery list will evolve effortlessly in this manner. At the store, if you find yourself grabbing a needed item not on the list, add it.

Step 6. Tweak your list weekly until it provides an accurate reflection of your own cooking needs. Of the 50,000 items available, you'll be taking home 20-60 each week. Your list will be like no one else's, but it will work for you and that's all that really matters.

Step 7. As soon as you take down one list, print and post a new one. Never be without a current shopping list posted in clear view.

If you continue to run out of needed ingredients after starting this practice, make a note on your list to buy more of those items. Keep tweaking your list until you are consistently enjoying the freedom of having the ingredients you need, when you need them, in stock in your home food pantry.

Remember: You are your own manager *and* customer. Never let yourself run out of the ingredients you need to succeed.

Price Comparison Shopping

Ever increasing time pressures, rising gas prices, greater distances between stores (as grocery storesfail) and skyrocketing prices make comparison shopping a tricky proposition.

I recommend you do comparison shopping anytime you are traveling near the vicinity of a second store for some non-grocery related reason. If you don't have to spend gas money or extra minutes, you can definitely find more bargain buys at that second store. Of course, if you pick up additional items not on your list, you just blew your savings.

If you love comparison shopping, and have the time to do it with grocery store options nearby, then I recommend you choose a "home" store and create your master grocery list for that store's layout. Leave extra space on the list where you can add the current best prices. As you move from store to store, jot notes. When you return home, enter your updates onto your Master Shopping List document and print out the upcoming week's list to post.

In-Store Strategies

Entering a grocery store with your shopping list in hand is the first sign you are taking your food spending seriously. Supermarket managers are anxious to relieve you of as much of your income as they can; tempting and appealing silent sales pitches are everywhere throughout grocery stores and it is your assets they are targeting.

Unfortunately, resisting the impressive aisle-end displays is only your first step in protecting your discretionary dollars. Much thought has gone into every aspect of grocery store layout. Eye-level and easy-to-reach places are reserved for goods with the highest markups, while the more cost-effective choices are relegated to top or bottom shelves and are usually put in the center aisles, less obvious to the casual shopper.

Thanks to marketing geniuses, you will need to think of yourself as a strategic planner in a battle of sorts: you and your money on one side and the advertisements and store layouts on the other. Defend your hard-earned cash by limiting your purchases to items highlighted on your Master Shopping List.

The Bureau of Labor Statistics (www.BLS.gov) reports that the average married parent spends one to three hours a week shopping for groceries. The best and easiest way to spend less of your money on food is to spend less of your time in the store.

As you limit your grocery shopping trips to one per week, with list in hand, and stick to your list, you will save big bucks. In addition, when you master the concepts of making your own dry mixes (chapter 4) and substituting ingredients you have for any missing ingredient, you'll be on a roll, saving time and money like a pro.

Strategies for Winning the War at the Supermarket

Advertisers spend billions of dollars each year trying to get you to buy more of their products. You're up against big bucks and powerful marketing resources, but there are strategies you can use to beat the odds.

Consider All Brands.   Assuming that name brands contain higher-quality ingredients than generics is not necessarily accurate. Just because a brand-name product costs more does not guarantee it is tastier or healthier than another brand. The difference in price is often due to advertising costs, and not to any real difference in ingredients. Complicate this a bit more by realizing that some generics now sell for more than their name brand counterparts. Basically, unless there's a taste difference, just use your pocket calculator and pick the most economical option.

Be Careful with Coupons.   Cents-off coupons are simply another form of advertising. They encourage shoppers, as do TV commercials, to purchase products they had not previously planned on buying. Before using a coupon, ask yourself two questions:

1. Would I have bought this if I didn't have a coupon? If the answer is no, it's not a good deal for you.
2. Does the math make sense? Find out by subtracting the price of the coupon from the cost of the advertised product. Compare that figure to the best deal you can get and buy the product or toss the coupon according to your findings.

Resist Attractive Packaging.   Another marketing strategy involves the actual packaging of processed foods.

I get a kick out of the photos on the box covers of frozen dinners. Don't they look appetizing? If you are a regular frozen dinner consumer, you will understand my amusement: What you see is rarely what you get.

Ready-to-heat dinners tend to cost more than twice their equivalent versions prepared at home. This would not be so bad, although a significant cost over time, if the ingredients were less adulterated with fillers such as starch, sauces, breading, and thickeners. The breading in heat-and-serve chicken dinners accounts for nearly 40 percent of the weight of the small pieces. Frozen egg rolls need to contain only 10 percent meat to meet United States Food Standards; chicken chow mein needs to contain only 4 percent meat. Better and less expensive versions of each of these products can be found in this book.

Build a Better Breakfast.   A major sinkhole for unsuspecting shoppers is the cold cereal section. Advertisers would have us believe that the most nutritious way to start our day is with these packages of, and I quote, "corn, sugar, salt, corn syrup, malt syrup, and annatto extract color." Of course, "BHT is added to preserve freshness," and the vitamins and minerals are stripped out in the production process.

Many cereals cost more per pound than fine steak, and none less per pound than chicken. Nutritious options such as toast, peanut butter, and juice allow you to sleep just as late and pocket a couple hundred bucks a year, depending on how much you buy now, of course. Chapter 10 lists some of my favorite breakfast recipes and shortcuts for fast, easy, and fun day-starters.

Stock Up on Meat before Holidays.   Most stores offer deep discounts on turkey the week just before Thanksgiving. Ham and turkey go on sale prior to Christmas, and bargains on steak, ground beef and brats can be found the week coming up to Memorial Day and other summer holidays. Your part of the country may have additional seasonal sales; when you see them come around, if you have freezer space, stock up. Frozen meat keeps for up to six months.

Buy Food and Household Products in Bulk.   Sam's Club was a fairly new concept in 1996, and buying groceries at Walmart or Target super stores was unheard of. Today, buying bulk is normal. We all do it, and, if you don't, you should. It makes good sense to stock up on items you know you will use when they are at their lowest price point.

The switch to bulk buying might require some creative thinking about one's storage situation. My own solution was to have a set of storage shelves built under the stairwell in our home and to put a spare freezer in the laundry room. Yours may be to turn the hall closet into a pantry. Wherever you put your bargains, you will gain both freedom and control by creating a pantry stocked with foods and household staples you know you will use.

I stock at least one extra "unit" of each nonperishable item on my Master Shopping List, and store or freeze larger quantities of foods that go on super sales. When I open my replacement or notice my supplies dwindling, I highlight the ingredient on my Master Shopping List. When shopping time arrives, my list is ready. There is no time wasted deciding what I need before I walk out the door.

One of the most exciting discoveries I made during my trek toward food freedom was the realization that maintaining a stocked pantry gives me the freedom to make anything in my recipe collection anytime I want. Gone is the discouragement of having to rule out numerous menu ideas simply because I'm missing one or more of the ingredients and don't have the time, energy, or money to go to the store again.

As you incorporate these strategies into your lifestyle, you will notice a decrease in food spending, an increase in free time, and a definite sense of being prepared. It is a great feeling to know that no matter what meal is ahead, or who may join you at the last minute to share it, you are equipped to make any recipe that comes to mind.

Funny Kitchen Moments with Marnie

Meals on Wheels

I had prepared a meal to send home with a friend whose family was returning from a medical trip. They were planning to stop by the house on their way through town to pick it up. Needing to leave for a few minutes, I instructed my 11-year-old son as follows:

"Mark, I need to run an errand. If Nancy stops by, tell her the dinner's in the fridge."

Upon my return, I asked, "Mark, did Nancy stop by?"

He said, "Yep! She was looking for you."

I said, "Did you tell her to look in the fridge?"

He replied with a funny look on his face, "No! Why would you be in the fridge?"

Restaurant Fun

Favorite Customer Complaint.

"I've tried your beef soft shell taco three times now, and I still don't like it!" Note: This taco is our number one best seller; we sell well over 10,000 a year to customers, some of whom drive miles out of their way for that specific taste.

Favorite Customer Order.

"I'd like a taco salad; no lettuce, please."

Favorite Health Inspection Write-Up.

"Too clean."

Favorite Employee Blooper.

"Thank you! Pull ahead, ma'am." Spoken to a customer standing at the counter; we don't even have a drive thru window.

warm water and add a squirt of dish soap. Cover and whir on high for about a minute, then rinse, and invert.

Master Your Microwave

Did you know that you can bring a stick of butter to room temperature by microwaving it on high for 8-10 seconds? Microwaves are awesome for quick cooking, thawing, and reheating plus many other time-consuming jobs.

If needed, a conventional oven recipe can be microwaved if you start checking for doneness after approximately a quarter of the suggested cooking time. For example, if a recipe calls for sixty minutes in the oven (regardless of temperature), start checking after fifteen minutes in the microwave. Continue cooking, checking often, and rotating your dish a quarter turn each time you check, until it is done. Make a note of how long it actually takes for future reference.

Besides reducing baking times, the microwave offers numerous shortcuts to otherwise boring or messy tasks.

- Spare yourself a dirty pan by sautéing onions in the microwave. Place 1/2 cup diced onions and 1 tablespoon butter in a microwave-safe dish; cover and cook on high for 2 to 3 minutes, stirring after each minute.
- Cook corn on the cob by placing unhusked ears on a paper towel in the microwave. Cook on high for 3 to 4 minutes per ear (or 10 to 11 minutes for four ears). Remove with pot holders and slide off husks and silk.
- Scald milk in a glass measuring cup on high. It takes just over 2 minutes per cup of milk.
- Melt marshmallow cream on high for 30 to 45 seconds per 7 ounces jar.
- Defrost 8 ounces of whipped topping on medium for 1 minute.
- Crisp stale pretzels, snack chips or crackers on high for 30 seconds; let stand 1 minute before serving.

- Soften rolls by wrapping each in a napkin or paper towel and microwaving on medium low for 15 to 30 seconds. Serve immediately.
- Maintain a moisture-proof environment to melt chocolate chips or squares without caking. Cook on high for 1 minute, stir vigorously, and microwave for additional 30-second intervals, stirring well between each, until smooth.
- Soften butter or cream cheese on high for 15 seconds per 4 ounces.
- Toast coconut until golden by cooking on high for 1 to 2 minutes.
- Roast nuts on high for 3 to 4 minutes, stirring after each 60-second interval.
- Soften lumpy brown sugar by microwaving it with a slice of bread in a covered dish on high for 30 to 60 seconds.
- Dry fresh herbs between layers of paper toweling by microwaving on high for 2 to 3 minutes. Let rest for 3 minutes and test to see if they are dry to the touch. If not, microwave at additional 30-second increments until dry.
- Crisp 4 slices of bacon between paper towels on high for 3 minutes.
- Defrost a loaf of frozen bread dough by placing in inside a plastic bag and microwaving it on high for 1 minute. Let stand for 2 minutes, rotate, and microwave for an additional 30 seconds. Portions of the dough will toughen if overcooked. Let the dough rest at room temperature for a few minutes, check again, and microwave at additional 10- to 15-second intervals until thawed.

Four Sample Timesaving, Quick-and-Easy Recipes

Your family has recipes that everyone enjoys week in and week out, month after month. The following sample recipes are a few of our favorite old standbys, and you may find they work in your home too. If you like the idea of having numerous choices at your fingertips, search online for "10 Minute Meals" or "Quick to Fix Recipes". There are literally millions. Narrow it down by adding to your list of search words a few of the main ingredients you have on hand or for which you are hungry. Every time you find a winner, add it to your Kitchen Notebook for easy access later.

Turkey Salsa Quickies

Use deli turkey or leftovers for this 3-minute meal.

Ingredients	Quantity	X____
Turkey meat, cooked and diced	1 cup	
Salsa (page 106)	2 cups	
Sour cream	1 cup	
Tortillas	8	
Shredded cheddar cheese	1/4 cup	
Yield	8	

Combine the meat, salsa, and sour cream. Layer some of the mixture in the center of each tortilla, then roll (log-style) and place, seam side down, in a glass baking dish. Cover with plastic wrap and microwave on high for 3 minutes, sprinkle with cheddar cheese, and microwave uncovered for an additional 30 seconds, until cheese melts.

Optional: Garnish with sour cream and diced onion, tomato, and lettuce.

Yorkshire Strata

Served with a pretty fruit salad, the soufflé frame and Worcestershire gravy turn otherwise boring leftovers into a very impressive dinner.

Ingredients	Quantity	X____
Cooked meat	1 cup	
Cooked, diced vegetables	1/2 cup	
Water	1/2 cup	
Beef or chicken gravy (recipe 61)	1-1/2 cups	
Worcestershire	1 Tablespoon	
Onion powder	1 teaspoon	
Butter	2 Tablespoons	
Milk	1 cup	
Eggs	2	
Flour	1 cup	
Salt	1/4 teaspoon	
Pepper	1/8 teaspoon	
Yield	6 to 8 servings	

Combine meat, vegetables, water, 1/4 cup of the gravy, Worcestershire, and onion powder; set aside. Place butter in a 10" pie plate and set in cold oven. Turn heat to 425°F.

In a blender container, combine milk, eggs, flour, salt, and pepper; blend on high for 45 seconds. Remove the hot pie plate and pour in the batter. Spoon meat mixture into center, leaving at least 1 inch around the edges. Return pie to oven for 30 minutes (do not open oven door). Remove directly to table where guests are waiting. Serve with heated gravy.

Fridge Biscuit Entrées

Inexpensive refrigerator biscuits offer speedy dinner options that kids and grown-ups enjoy.

Press individual biscuits into 10 greased muffin tins, making a well in the center of each. Fill the wells with one of the following:

- A combination of browned ground meat and BBQ sauce topped with a few sprinkles of cheddar cheese.

- A combination of condensed cream of chicken soup or gravy plus leftover turkey or chicken meat plus leftover peas or carrots, topped with a few sprinkles of cheddar cheese.

- A combination of diced ham and blender-puréed cottage cheese, topped with cheddar cheese.

Freeze until firm, then transfer to an airtight container for later use, or bake at 425°F for 10 minutes and serve hot.

Another great option is to roll out biscuits with a rolling pin and let kids make their own mini-pizzas with ingredients of their choice. Freeze or bake at 425°F for 8 to 10 minutes.

Note: All of the above filling options, once heated through, serve up nicely inside pita bread, a tortilla or two slices of toast.

Super Quick BBQ Sauce

Ingredients	Quantity	X4
Ketchup	1/2 cup	2 cups
Brown sugar	1/4 cup	1 cup
Liquid smoke	1/4 teaspoon	1 teaspoon
Garlic powder	1/4 teaspoon	1 teaspoon
Yield	1/2 cup	2 cups

Mix well. Brush over ready-to-grill meat, serve as a dip or combine with one pound browned ground beef or pork and serve on buns.

Susan's Poppy Chicken

This recipe comes from my good friend, Susan Helweg. This awesome cook is the mother of eleven and the grandmother of an ever-growing number of lucky little grandchildren.

Ingredients	Quantity	X ____
Chicken meat, cooked and diced	2-1/2 cups	
Cream of chicken soup	10 ounce can	
Sour Cream	1 cup	
Ritz crackers, crushed	1 cup	
Butter, melted	1 stick	
Poppyseed	1 Tablespoon	
Yield	9x9" casserole	

Mix first 3 ingredients and layer into a 9x9" casserole. Mix together remaining ingredients and sprinkle over meat mixture. Bake at 350°F for 20 minutes. Serve with pasta, rice, potatoes or toast.

Chapter 3

One Mess, Many Meals

*Making one meal at a time is
as silly as putting one gallon of gas
in your car per station visit.*

In this chapter you will learn how to maximize your kitchen minutes to…

- fill your freezer with your family's favorite ready-to-heat entrées, sides and desserts in the minutes you were going to spend in the kitchen anyway.
- spend less time cooking yet find yourself more frequently serving homemade meals.
- save money on food every time you drive by fast food options. You'll do this often when you know you've got a healthy quick-to-fix meal waiting for you at home.
- go green by saving water (washing less dishes) and saving electricity (maximizing your freezer space), all with this one kitchen strategy.
- turn every mess into multiple meals.

Have you ever made two of something with the express intent to serve one now and freeze the other for later?

Have you ever taken something frozen out, only to find it has freezer burn, tin foil that's been "eaten through" by the food inside it, or heated something up with soggy or disappointing results?

Mastering the art of cooking in bulk makes sense, but there are some clear and important "do's and don'ts" that can make or break your bulk cooking experience. This chapter contains the simple strategies that will help you be a success every single time.

From today forward, whenever you take the time to make a family favorite, maximize those minutes to gift yourself with a few extra fast meals for the super busy days in your future.

Expansion cooking makes good sense. If you are going to mess up the kitchen and spend your precious moments preparing a made-from-scratch dish, why not make more than one?

Even if you have limited pans, mixing bowls, and utensils, you can make your own convenient frozen dinners at a fraction of what you would pay for highly processed ones from the supermarket. In addition, the knowledge of their presence in your freezer will enable you to drive by every money-sucking, high fat, fast food option on your way home from a hectic day.

The following list of hints and tips should convince you that cooking in quantity can truly expand your time and budget.

THE HOWS AND WHYS OF COOKING IN QUANTITY	
HERE'S HOW	HERE'S WHY
• For huge batches, make use of electric skillets, Dutch ovens, and Crock-Pots.	• You can make a lot more food in the same amount of time by taking advantage of these additional cooking appliances.
• Keep your freezer at 0°F.	• This is a safe temperature for all frozen foods.
• Slightly undercook noodles, rice, and potatoes that are to be frozen and reheated later.	• They have a tendency to dry out if overcooked.

HERE'S HOW	HERE'S WHY
• If using tomato sauce, do not precook the pasta. Be sure the noodles are completely covered with sauce. This works well for spaghetti, lasagna, manicotti, etc.	• The sauce will separate slightly in freezing and the noodles will cook in the water while baking. Excess water is absorbed, yielding a thick, rich sauce.
• Ground meat can be browned, drained, and frozen on cookie sheets until firm, then transferred to freezer-quality bags and returned to the freezer.	• This allows meat to be measured out in exact amounts as needed and requires less time to thaw.
• When freezing layered dishes like lasagna, place a large enough piece of heavy-duty aluminum foil in your baking dish to allow you to fold it over the top. Assemble the ingredients as directed, seal tightly, and freeze in pan. When frozen, pop out the foil package, label and date it, and return the entrée to the freezer until needed. To use, slip off the tin foil jacket under warm running water and place the frozen entrée in the original baking dish. Cook as directed.	• This technique allows you to prepare numerous entrées ahead of time without investing in additional baking dishes. Also, the foil packages take up much less space in the freezer than do pans and casserole dishes.
• Use freezer-quality zip-top bags when possible. Layered dishes require above treatment, but most other foods freeze well in zip-tops.	• These bags hold more food than seems possible. They also freeze flat and take up much less room in your freezer.

HERE'S HOW	HERE'S WHY
• Reuse freezer-quality bags until they get a hole; then discard.	• These bags are expensive but durable. A single hole in a bag can ruin an entire dinner. Check for holes while washing.
• Do not freeze foods in wax paper, regular aluminum foil, or regular zip-top bags.	• These substances are not durable enough for freezing purposes.
• Label packages well. Include entrée name, date assembled and cooking instructions.	• Meals have a tendency to look alike once frozen. Including use instructions saves you looking it up later.
• Use masking tape to seal packages.	• Costs less than freezer tape and works better than transparent tapes.
• When you are making two or more batches of an entrée, do similar tasks all at once. For example, place the first layer of noodles in all the pans, then the first layer of sauce in all pans, etc.	• This saves time and mental energy because it requires that you read the recipe only once and you do each preparation task only once.

HERE'S HOW	HERE'S WHY
• Refreeze meat or prepared foods only if you have altered their consistency by cooking. In other words, do not thaw a pound of hamburger, make meatballs, and return the meatballs to the freezer unless you have cooked the meat. If you want to make a big batch of meatballs without cooking them, prepare the meatballs while the ground beef is still fresh.	• Reduces risk of freezer burn and rancidity.
• Unless you are very familiar with your microwave's defrost functions, avoid defrosting frozen entrées in the microwave.	• Most microwaves start cooking portions of the entrée before the entire entrée is even thawed.

More Secrets for Successful Cooking in Quantity

Main Dish Magic   Whether your part of the country calls it a casserole, covered dish or hotdish, the most obvious recipes to expand are main dish entrées that include noodles or rice. Assemble the extra meals while you are making tonight's dinner, but freeze them before baking. When you cook them immediately prior to use, the aroma and fresh taste will make guests think the dish was just assembled. The recipe for Layered Tamale Pie (page 39) is one of our favorite expandable casserole entrées. Since this is a layered dish, I use the tip about lining extra baking dishes or bowls of similar size with heavy-duty aluminum foil for the extra meals. To expedite assembly, I place the bottom tortilla in each dish, then a layer of sauce in each, and continue in assembly-line fashion as directed.

One note about freezing cheddar cheese: If it comes in contact with aluminum foil it can actually eat a hole in the foil. To avoid this, wait to add the shredded cheese until just before you bake the dish.

Two more layered dishes that are easy to prepare, freeze well, and taste great when thawed and cooked are Spaghetti Pie (page 40) and Layered Turkey Bake (page 41).

If a recipe you wish to increase does not provide instructions for reheating from frozen, use this basic rule: Remove the dish from the freezer wrapping and place it, still frozen, in a covered casserole dish in a cold over. Turn the oven to 350°F and bake for approximately half again the originally recommended cooking time (for example, if the recipe calls for 30 minutes baking time, bake it for 45 minutes), uncovering the dish halfway through. Test for doneness by feeling a knife that has been inserted into the center of the casserole. If the knife comes out hot, the dish is done. If not, recover the casserole and keep cooking. Unless otherwise noted, most casserole dishes keep nicely in the freezer for up to six months.

Freezing Meats, Poultry, and Fish   There is no need to limit your expanding activities to casseroles; fried or broiled meat and poultry pieces are also excellent freezer options. Divide the portions you wish to save into serving-size, freezer-quality containers; label and refreeze for up to six months. Thaw in the refrigerator and serve cold, or unwrap while still frozen and place in a 350°F oven until heated through. The time will vary significantly with the thickness of your meat, so check it frequently.

Cooked sliced meats are another freezable option if they are covered completely with a sauce or gravy. Thaw in the refrigerator and reheat in a covered baking dish at 350°F for 30 to 60 minutes.

For whole, sliced, or slivered ham and turkey ham, simply divide into serving-size quantities, place in zip-top bags, and freeze for up to 3 months without added sauces or gravy. Thaw in the refrigerator overnight, drain excess liquid, and prepare as desired.

One of my favorite meals to make and serve is Sunday's roast beef dinner. It's a super easy meal. I always cook more than enough so we can invite last minute guests or use the leftovers to make beef stew, beef stroganoff, or slice and heat sandwich meat.

Roast for Sunday lunch is a family tradition that both my parents and Dave's passed along to us. Our kids never tired of roast, potatoes, gravy, and carrots on Sundays and neither have we.

My family and I live just one mile from Lake of the Woods on the Canadian border and we take advantage of the fishing. When the fish are biting, we sometimes bring home more than we can eat all at once. If I am going to do a fish fry, including the mess of hot oil, I make the most of it. I fry up every last filet (see Incredible Fried Fish on page 83-84) and then freeze the leftovers in freezer-quality zip-top bags for excellent fishwiches—fish fillets served between hamburger buns with Tartar Sauce (page 201).

Freezer Solutions for pizza, soup, stew, stuffing, snacks & desserts Homemade pizzas are always in demand. Assemble extra pizzas, wrap well, label, and freeze until needed. To cook, place the unwrapped frozen pizza on a baking sheet and bake at 425°F for 15 to 20 minutes. Uncooked pizzas will keep in the freezer for up to 1 month, although a lock on your freezer door may be the only way to accomplish that feat!

Soups and stews freeze well if you avoid potatoes and slightly undercook the vegetables and noodles. There are several mix-and-match soup options in this book that make it easy. If you wish to freeze a cream soup, plan to add some thickener when until you reheat the combination. To serve, heat from frozen in a heavy saucepan over low heat. As it thaws, break apart the main chunk with a fork. Add thickeners and any additional seasonings as required; heat through, and serve.

Stuffing is a great side dish and keeps well in the freezer for up to 1 month. If left in a cooked turkey, stuffing can be unsafe, so remove all of the stuffing before proceeding with your other dinner responsibilities. Any leftover stuffing should be cooled to room temperature, placed in freezer-quality containers, labeled, and frozen. Later, unwrap and bake in a covered casserole dish at 350°F for 20 minutes. Remove the cover and continue baking for 10 minutes longer. If you enjoy the convenience of boxed stuffing mixes, you can save a small fortune and turn out superior stuffing every time with the recipe for Seasoned Stuffing Mix on (page 74).

Expand your horizons even further by creating exciting fruit side dishes in quantity. I keep a large supply of Frosty Fruit Cups (page 124) in the freezer and call on them often to round out a variety of meals. Fancy and festive, they work well for breakfast, brunch, or dinner.

Be sure to include desserts in your expanding repertoire. Frozen desserts keep for months and offer great comfort when unexpected guests arrive on your doorstep. One of the crowd pleasers at our house is Frozen Mud Pie (page 150).

Snacks and treats also freeze well. You can make your own slice-and-bake cookie dough using your favorite recipe and a plastic wrap box to create a mold for the dough. Tear off a large piece of wrap and then remove the tube from the box. Use the wrap you just tore off to line the empty plastic wrap box and spoon in the cookie dough, creating a tube of dough. Seal and label each roll. Store in the refrigerator for up to 3 weeks, or in the freezer for up to 6 months.

If you enjoy frozen snacks on a stick, make your own fruit pops for extra nutrition and variety. One of our favorite family recipes is found on page 142.

Freezer Do's and Don'ts

While most foods freeze well and are suitable for expanding, the chart below gives the exceptions and the reasons why you should avoid freezing these particular ingredients. For certain foods—such as cream cheese and cottage cheese—I give the caution because the food sometimes separates when thawed. In dishes such as lasagna, separation is hard to detect, but for something like cheesecake, separated cream cheese would ruin your presentation.

FREEZER HINTS	
DO NOT FREEZE	**BECAUSE**
• Cooked egg whites or hard-cooked eggs	• They may become rubbery.
• Salad dressing or mayonnaise	• It may separate.
• Milk sauces	• They may curdle.
• Carbonated beverages	• They may explode as they expand. Even if they don't explode, they may be flat when thawed.
• Meringue	• It may shrink and ooze.
• Cream or cottage cheese	• It may separate or break down.
• Hard cheese (I freeze any cheese that will be crumbled or shredded for use on pizzas, casseroles, etc. Hard cheese may be frozen in blocks or already shredded.)	• It crumbles when cut.
• Yogurt or sour cream	• It may separate.
• Fresh salad ingredients	• They wilt when thawed.

DO NOT FREEZE	BECAUSE
• Gelatins or gelatin desserts	• They get runny.
• Creams or custards	• They become watery and lumpy and may separate.

If you are taking advantage of bulk purchasing and expansion cooking, the possibility of power failure carries with it the threat of wiping out a lot of food and effort. Here are some tips that should provide a little peace of mind should an outage occur, including the reasons why each is valuable.

FREEZER ADVICE FOR A POWER OUTAGE	
INSTRUCTION	REASON
• Keep your freezer door shut.	• A fully packed freezer will keep food frozen for 48 hours or more if the door is never opened.
• Order sliced dry ice and place it in the freezer. Use cardboard to keep the ice from coming into contact with the food.	• This will keep food frozen.
• Refreeze foods that are still firm or have ice crystals on them.	• These foods have not suffered damage.
• Cook and serve, or cook, repackage and refreeze foods that are cool or partially thawed.	• These foods would probably get freezer burn if refrozen in their original form.

3 Sample Breeze-to-Freeze Recipes

Layered Tamale Pie

Ingredients	Quantity	X4
Ground beef	1 pound	4 pounds
Black olives	4 ounces	1 pound
Tomato sauce	15 ounces	3.5 pounds
Taco seasoning mix (page 65)	1 package	4 packages
Corn tortillas (small)	6	24
Water	1/3 cup	1-1/3 cup
Yield	4 servings	16 servings

Combine meat, diced olives, tomato sauce, and seasonings. Place one corn tortilla in bottom of a greased 10" round casserole. Layer on sauce, another tortilla, sauce, tortilla, etc., ending with sauce. Sprinkle with cheddar cheese and then pour the water around edges of casserole. Freeze or bake covered at 400°F for 40 minutes. Let stand before cutting.

From frozen: Place covered, frozen entrée in cold oven. Turn heat to 375°F and bake for 60 minutes.

Spaghetti Pie

Ingredients	Quantity	X2
Angel hair pasta, cooked	6 ounces	10 ounces
Butter	1 Tablespoon	1 Tablespoon
Parmesan cheese	1/4 cup	1/3 cup
Eggs, beaten	2	3
Cottage cheese	3/4 cup	1-1/2 cups
Ground beef, browned and drained	1/2 pound	1 pound
Spaghetti sauce seasoning mix (page 67)	1 package (2 teaspoons)	2 packages
Tomato paste	6 ounces	12 ounces
Water	1 cup	1-1/2 cups
Yield	9" round	9x13" pan

Combine drained pasta, butter, cheese, and eggs. Mix well and form a shell in a 9" round or 9x13" pan. Set aside. In blender container, whir cottage cheese on high until smooth. Spoon it onto the noodle crust. Combine ground beef, seasonings, tomato paste, and water; mix well. Spoon oven cottage cheese. Freeze or bake at 350°F for 35 minutes. Garnish with Parmesan or cheddar cheese if desired.

From frozen: Place frozen pie in cold over. Turn oven to 350°F and bake for 60 minutes.

Note: Noodles must be precooked for this recipe since the sauce does not cover them completely.

Layered Turkey Bake

Ingredients	Quantity	X2
Seasoned stuffing mix (page 74)	2 cups	4 cups
Butter	2 Tablespoons	4 Tablespoons
Water	1/2 cup	1 cup
Eggs, beaten	1	2
Chicken/turkey meat, cooked and diced	2 cups	4 cups
Cream of chicken soup (page 58)	1-1/4 cups	2-1/2 cups
Milk	1 cup	2 cups
Yield	8" pan	9x13" pan

Combine stuffing, butter, and water. Layer half of mixture in bottom of an 8x8" or 9x13" pan. Mix together eggs and meat and spoon this on top of base layer. Cover with second half of stuffing mixture. Combine soup and milk and stir well. Pour over all and freeze, or cover and bake at 350°F for 35 to 45 minutes.

From frozen: Place covered frozen entrée in 350°F oven and bake for 50 to 60 minutes.

Finding More Easy-to-Freeze Recipes

Your own recipe collection is full of freezable options and a simple Google search using the search words, "make ahead meal," yields over 4 million results. Refine your search by adding the key ingredients to the search string. Thus, if you need to use up some ground beef, cheddar cheese, and mushrooms, you would search for, "make ahead meal, ground beef, cheddar, mushroom." This string yields 400,000 options.

A Few Favorite Online Food Related Sites

http://www.AllRecipes.com   Enjoy thousands of well-organized recipes that feature star ratings letting you know what others thought after making that recipe.

http://www.Recipe.com   Being a visual person, I love the step-by-step photos found at this massive site. Recipe.com shows user rankings with forks instead of stars. Fun idea!

http://www.theEpiCentre.com   This is my favorite spice dictionary online. If a recipe calls for a spice I don't have (or don't recognize), I visit the EpiCenter. I either find a substitution that will work in my recipe, or the reason why one won't.

http://homecooking.about.com   Home Cooking Guide, Peggy Trowbridge Filippone, is my online go-to girl for so many, many things related to home cooking. You'll love her!

Jessie Weaver is a stay-at-home mom, writer & editor who hosts a blog at http://www.vanderbiltwife.com. Doing a quick search for "Make Ahead Meals," I found her site. Here is one of the fun recipes she shares there.

Breakfast Burritos to Freeze: Pile scrambled eggs, cheese, sausage, bacon, tomatoes, spinach or any of your own favorites into a burrito. Fold, seal in plastic wrap and freeze individually. Unwrap and microwave about 2-2.5 minutes.

Chapter 4

Dry Mix Magic

This strategy gives you the ability
to create your own dry mixes,
at home, anytime, with less sodium,
no additives and with cost savings of 50-90%.

Of the vast collection of modern convenience foods, my favorites are dry package mixes. The simplicity of ripping open an envelope compared to the mess of chopping and measuring is obvious, and food manufacturers use this fact to their advantage.

Did you know that the Ranch Dressing Mix recipe on page 135 costs less than a tenth of the supermarket price when you make the dry mix at home? If you buy Shake & Bake, you might be surprised to learn that you can coat the same thirty-two pieces of chicken for less than 10 percent of what you would pay in the store (recipe on page 68).

The key to saving money and time is to measure out big batches of your favorites. Unlike prepackaged mixes, home versions contain only a few ingredients, all of which are pronounceable and most of which are without additives.

Start Your Own Collection of Homemade Dry Mixes

There is an easy way to develop a pantry full of homemade convenience foods at a fraction of the cost of the store-bought equivalents.

Throughout this chapter you'll find many of my own favorite dry mix recipes. Any time you are going to make a meal using a dry mix, take advantage of your time in the kitchen and the fact that you already have all the ingredients out on the counter to make a big batch. Measure the quantity for tonight's dinner into one bowl, and the larger quantity into another. Once your dinner is assembled and cooking, take a moment to write a label including the name of the mix, the date you assembled it, and how to use it. You will soon have a cupboard full of dry mix options that will save you a fortune, using the minutes you were already in the kitchen.

If creating a dry mix collection all at once suits you better, start by flagging the recipes you want to assemble. Make sure you have the required ingredients on hand and arrange them and all needed measuring utensils and storage containers on your counter. Assemble one mix after another until your dry mix collection is complete—all in one session.

Use moisture-proof, airtight, containers with good seals or tight-fitting lids. Practically any clean container with a tight-fitting lid would offer suitable storage; some of my favorites include sour cream and cottage cheese containers. For large batches, I use clean, dry, ice-cream buckets or other plastic or deli containers. For small batches, I prefer freezer-quality zip-top bags. An empty shoe box or other similar-sized container works well as a "file cabinet" for dry mixes in zip-tops. Of course, you should never use a container that has previously contained a harmful substance, even if you wash it out.

Label your mixes as you prepare them. They will look alike later, so do it immediately. I prefer self-adhesive labels, available from office supply stores, but writing on masking tape works, and even on a square of paper with the name of the mix, date when assembled, and use instructions written on it can be taped to your container for quick identification. However you decide to do it, be sure to do it as you go.

For no-fuss cooking, I place additional labels on the exterior of large batch containers, including instructions for the recipes I use most often that involve that mix. Later I just grab the container and cook from those instructions instead of hauling out a cookbook. Once I have a storage container labeled, I use it over and over for the same mix, thus eliminating relabeling. Since these are dry mixes, I just wipe the inside with a damp cloth, dry it out, and let it sit until the next assembly session.

Mass quantity dry mix assembly will go more quickly if you use two sets of measuring utensils: one for dry ingredients and the other for shortening. I keep a few paper towels handy to wipe out opposing flavors like pepper and sugar, but I do not clean between flavors that more or less blend.

When measuring shortening (which happens repeatedly during a major assembly session), try this trick. If you need 2 cups of shortening, pour 2 cups cold water into a 4-cup glass measure. Spoon the shortening into the water, pressing down as needed to keep it submerged, until the water/shortening combination increases the volume to 4 cups. Hold a few fingers over the shortening, invert the cup over the sink, drain the water, and you are left with exactly 2 cups of shortening without the sticking or air pockets that so frustrate an otherwise smooth assembly process. If you need only 1/2 cup shortening, pour 2 cups cold water into the measuring cup, add shortening until the total comes to the 2-1/2-cup level, pour off the water, and there is your 1/2 cup.

If you want to make a big batch of a dry mix recipe, but you have never tried the recipe and are not sure you will like it, simply make your "trial" recipe and leave out all the dry ingredients until after you have taste-tested the final product. If it passes the test, quickly measure out your big batch, label it, and save time and money from now on! If not, then put the ingredients away and you will have wasted no time or ingredients at all.

This final assembly tip can be a lifesaver if interruptions are common in your home. When a recipe requires, let us say, 8 cups of flour, place 8 tokens (coins, pens, whatever is handy) in front of the flour canister. As you measure, move the tokens, one for each cup, to the other side of the mixing bowl. Even if the phone rings or your toddler spills his milk, you will know exactly how much flour you still need to add.

The time savings available with dry mixes is exciting! If you have some traditional recipes you make repeatedly, consider rewriting them to take advantage of this. I rewrote my chili recipe (which we loved but I didn't make too often because it required time-consuming chopping and dicing). Now I can throw it together in seconds and it tastes great. I'll show you how I did it farther on.

Before you consider rewriting one of your own favorites, be sure to check the "Dry Mix" heading in the index to see if I have already done the work for you. I've included several in this chapter and more in the Substitutions and Equivalents Guide (SEG) beginning on page 165. If your favorite is not on the list, check the Internet and bombs away!

The first step is to decide if your recipe would be more cost effective and/or less time consuming in dry mix format. The SEG at the end of this book will help you identify how many of the fresh or liquid ingredients in the recipe can be changed to dry, room-temperature substitutes.

This is how my favorite brownie recipe appeared in its original form:

Marnie's Favorite Brownie Mix (Before)

3/4 cup sugar

1 cup flour

1/2 teaspoon salt

4 eggs, slightly beaten

10 Tablespoons butter, melted

12 ounces chocolate chips, melted

2 teaspoons vanilla

Mix and spread all ingredients in greased 9x13" pan. Bake at 350°F for 30 minutes.

The only dry ingredients listed in the original recipe are sugar, flour, and salt, but the SEG shows that you can replace the butter with butter-flavored shortening, which has a shelf life of six months. The chocolate chips can be replaced with unsweetened cocoa and extra sugar and butter-flavored shortening. The only remaining ingredients are eggs and vanilla. Here is the revised recipe with a few other changes I will explain in a moment:

Brownie Mix (After)

Ingredients	Quantity	X4
Flour	1 cup	4 cups
Sugar	2 cups	8 cups
Unsweetened cocoa	3/4 cup	3 cups (8 ounces)
Salt	1/2 teaspoon	2 teaspoons
Shortening	1 cup	4 cups
Yield	4-1/2 cups	18 cups

Combine dry ingredients; cut in shortening. Store in moisture-proof, airtight containers at room temperature for up to 6 months.

Use Instructions:	Small	Original
Eggs	2	4
Vanilla	1 teaspoon	1 teaspoon
Dry mix	2-1/4 cups	4-1/2 cups
Chopped nuts/coconut	1/2 cup	1 cup
Yield	12 brownies	24 brownies

Combine eggs and vanilla, beat until foamy. Add dry mix and stir until well blended. Pour into an 8x8" or 9x13" pan. Bake at 350°F for 25 minutes. Cool and serve plain or frosted.

Useful Hints for Making Your Own Dry Mixes

You may have noticed that the ingredient lists in all my recipes are arranged in reverse order: ingredient on the left, quantity on the right. This allows you to see at a glance which ingredients to assemble, and then to write in your own expanded or reduced quantities at will.

When I rewrite recipes, I often personalize them by changing quantities to make them more useful for me. For the "After" version of the brownie mix, I expanded the dry mix portion so I could make a big batch. As you adapt your recipes to meet your needs, each becomes more valuable. Write notes directly on them—they are not fine art. They are your tools, and writing on them, or at least adding sticky-notes, makes them more useful.

If the recipe you are converting uses shortening, remember to include instructions to cut it in after you finish combining the dry ingredients. Also, the shelf life should be noted as six months minus the number of months the shortening can was opened before the mix was assembled. For example, if you opened your shortening can in June and assembled your mix in September, you should make a note on the dry mix label indicating it will expire in December. Dry mixes assembled at home without shortening do not usually require expiration dates.

Once you decide which dry mix recipes you want to make in bulk, buy the predominant spices and seasonings required from a health food store or warehouse club like Sam's or Costco. Either way, you will save money on your main ingredients.

Also, as noted, unsweetened cocoa powder is a possible substitute for baking chips or chocolates. However, if your end product relies on the bonding agent in the chocolate chips or squares to help hold its shape, as in mousse or candy recipes, cocoa powder will not work.

Not all recipes are as conducive to dry mix revision as the brownies were. Crème de Menthe Syrup, for example, is one of my favorite toppings and adds a touch of class to so many desserts, but doesn't make sense as a dry mix. First, most of the ingredients cannot be translated into dry alternatives. Next, it takes just seconds to whip up, so there is no time-savings. Finally, either way, I save 60% off the store-bought version.

Crème de Menthe Syrup

Ingredients	Quantity	X____
Water	2/3 cup	
Light corn syrup	1/3 cup	
Peppermint extract	3/4 teaspoon	
Green food coloring	6 drops	
Yield	1 cup	

Stir all ingredients to combine and store indefinitely in an airtight container at room temperature.

If the recipe you are considering contains a majority of liquid ingredients even after you have exhausted every possible substitution, it is best to leave it in its original form.

Another favorite recipe, Sopaipillas, is ruled out as a dry mix because of its numerous steps. While I highly recommend these as impressive appetizers for a Mexican meal, the recipe is simply too complicated to be successfully converted to a dry mix. Here is the regular recipe.

Mexican Sopaipillas

Ingredients	Quantity	X____
Milk	1-1/2 cups	
Yeast	1 Tablespoon	
Flour	4 cups	
Baking powder	1 teaspoon	
Salt	1 teaspoon	
Butter	1 Tablespoon	
Oil for frying		
Yield	70 Sopaipillas	

Scald milk; let cool. Activate yeast in 1/2 cup warm water. Combine flour, baking powder, and salt; cut in butter. Add 1 cup of the cooled milk and the yeast mixture. Toss gently and add just enough of the remaining milk so dough holds together. Knead on lightly floured surface fifteen times. Proceed, cover and freeze, or refrigerate until needed. When ready to use, let (thawed dough) stand at room temperature for 10 minutes. Heat 4" oil to 375°F. Divide dough in half and roll first half to 1/4" inch thickness. Cut dough into 2-3 inches squares and drop each into hot oil, forcing under until puffed. Allow to brown on one side, flip, and hold under until golden. Remove to paper towels and serve hot with honey.

Marnie's Favorite Chili (Before)

At first glance, my chili recipe appeared to have too many fresh and liquid ingredients to convert to a dry mix.

1 pound ground beef

1/4 cup diced onion

1 small garlic clove

1-1/2 Tablespoons flour

1/2 teaspoon chili powder

1/4 teaspoon ground cumin

1/2 teaspoon salt

Drop of Tabasco sauce

15 ounces tomato sauce

1/2 cup water

1-15 ounce can kidney beans, not drained

Brown the ground beef, onion, and garlic; drain fat. Stir in remaining ingredients except beans. Simmer for 30 to 40 minutes, covered, stirring occasionally, until flavors blend. Add the beans and cook until heated through.

Here is the same recipe after substitutions were made.

Chili Seasoning Mix (After)

Ingredients	Quantity	X10
Flour	1-1/2 Tablespoons	1-1/8 cups
Onion flakes	1 Tablespoon	3/4 cup
Chili powder	1/2 teaspoon	3 Tablespoons
Salt	1/2 teaspoon	2 Tablespoons
Ground cumin	1/4 teaspoon	1 Tablespoon
Sugar	1/4 teaspoon	1 Tablespoon
Cayenne	Sprinkle	2 teaspoons
Garlic powder	Sprinkle	1/2 teaspoon
Yield	3 Tablespoons	30 Tablespoons

Combine all ingredients and store indefinitely in a moisture-proof, airtight container at room temperature.

Use Instructions:

Dry mix	3 Tablespoons
Ground beef, browned	1 pound
Tomato sauce	15 ounces
Water	1/2 cup
Kidney beans, including liquid	15 ounces
Yield (6 to 8 servings)	50 ounces (equivalent to 2 regular cans)

Combine all ingredients in a saucepan, bring to boil. Reduce heat and simmer for at least 20 minutes, covered. Stir often.

In this example, the chopping of onions and peeling of garlic cloves has been eliminated by conversion to garlic powder. The Tabasco sauce was converted to cayenne. All of the ingredients were then placed in order, with the dry ones listed first and the "last-minute" ones listed under them. With these simple revisions, the goodness of homemade chili is captured in an inexpensive, quickly assembled recipe.

When looking for ingredients to convert, remember that anything requiring refrigeration needs to be replaced by a room-temperature alternative. A few examples include substituting powdered milk for liquid, dry mustard for regular, or butter-flavored shortening for butter. Some substitutions, such as onion powder for onions, cayenne for Tabasco sauce, and sugar for honey may surprise you. Checking the SEG thoroughly ensures you will not miss any timesaving options.

Take care when dealing with seeds or flakes such as onion flakes, red pepper flakes, celery seeds, etc. When you use these flakes, it will take your recipe at least 20 minutes of simmering or 4 hours of refrigeration (for recipes like salad dressings or dips) to blend satisfactorily. If speed is paramount, opt for powders (such as onion powder, cayenne, celery salt, etc.) over flakes. Chili powder is the only powder that requires extra time: Simmer foods including this spice for at least 15 minutes for best results.

Most dry mix recipes can be increased or decreased without adverse effect. If you use large quantities of corn bread, for example, you may wish to assemble a big batch of dry mix. Do this by multiplying the base quantity of each ingredient by whatever number of mixes you are interested in making and then proceed as directed. It takes no longer to measure out 1/2 cup baking powder than it does to measure out 2 teaspoons, but by doing it all at once you will save time later. You can do something else during the time you would have spent taking out all the ingredients and measuring each one again (and again the next time, and the next time, and so on).

Corn Bread Mix

Ingredients	Quantity	X 2	X8
Flour	1 cup	2 cups	8 cups
Cornmeal	1/2 cup	1 cup	4 cups
Sugar	1/4 cup	1/2 cup	2 cups
Baking powder	2 teaspoons	4 teaspoons	3 Tablespoons
Salt	1/2 teaspoon	1 teaspoon	2 teaspoons
Yield	1-1/2 cups	3 cups	12 cups

Combine all ingredients and store indefinitely in a moisture-proof, airtight container at room temperature.

Use Instructions:

Dry mix	1-1/2 cups
Egg	1
Milk	1 cup
Oil	1/4 cup
Yield	12 muffins or 8x8" pan

Mix all ingredients until just blended. Pour into greased muffin tins, corn bread tins, or an 8x8" pan. Bake at 425°F: muffin or corn bread tins for 18 minutes; 8x8" pan for 20 to 24 minutes. Serve warm or freeze until needed.

You will notice that the yield of dry mix has been translated into the single batch amount under "Use Instructions." If you are rewriting a recipe, you will want to measure the quantity of your combined ingredients carefully and enter that figure on your recipe under "Yield". It is important to actually measure and not simply add up the total of all the individual ingredients to arrive at this number because powdered spices may "hide" between flaked onions, parsley, etc., and your figure may be off enough to ruin a dish.

To determine how much you need for each batch, divide the total yield by the number of times you multiplied the recipe. For example, if you multiplied the ingredients by 5, you will want to divide the total yield by 5 to determine the quantity required under Use instructions. Shake your mix well before you measure and also be sure to shake it up again immediately before you measure out the quantity needed for any given recipe.

To help me quickly increase or decrease amounts of any given ingredient, I created a chart I refer to as my Up-and-Down Chart (see next page). The figures are approximate, but I have used them for my own rewriting adventures for many years and feel confident they are close enough for this purpose. The Original column equals the amount called for in your original recipe. If you wish to make half a batch, use the figures under ".5"; if you wish to make a triple batch, use the figures under "3x", and so on.

A few other favorite charts appear in Appendix II, but I like to keep the Up-and-Down Chart with my dry mix assembly information for checking as I go. If super convenience interests you, make a photocopy of this chart and tape it inside one of your kitchen cupboard doors.

Finally, a word of caution regarding increasing spice quantities. Some spices, such as chili powder, pepper, and dry mustard, could ruin your mix if you multiply them up to the same degree as milder spices such as nutmeg, paprika, and onion powder. The recipes in this book show that multiplying up is safe in most instances. You will soon get a feel for how much spice you prefer in your mixes, but, until then, double the amount of questionable or strong spices called for in the original recipe only every third or fourth increase.

THE UP-AND-DOWN CHART

Approximate Figures

.25X	.33X	.5X	Original	2X	3X	4X	6
Sprinkle	Sprinkle	Sprinkle	1/8 tsp	1/4 tsp	3/8tsp	1/2 tsp	3/4tsp
Sprinkle	Sprinkle	1/8 tsp	1/4 tsp	1/2 tsp	3/4 tsp	1 tsp	
Sprinkle	1/8 tsp	1/4 tsp	1/2 tsp	1 tsp	1-1/2 tsp	2 tsp	
1/8 tsp	1/4 tsp	1/2 tsp	1 tsp	2 tsp	1 tbls	4tsp	
1/4 tsp	1/2 tsp	1 tsp	2 tsp	4tsp	2 tbls	8tsp	
1/2 tsp	3/4 tsp	1-1/2 tsp	1 tbls	2 tbls	3 tbls	1/4 cup	
1 tsp	2 tsp	1 tbls	2 tbls	1/4 cup	1/3 cup	1/2 cup	
1-1/2 tsp	1 tbls	2 tbls	1/4 cup	1/2 cup	3/4 cup	1 cup	
2 tsp	4 tsp	2-1/2 tbls	1/3 cup	2/3 cup	1 cup	1-1/2 cups	
1 tbls	2 tbls	1/4 cup	1/2 cup	1 cup	1-1/2 cups	2 cups	
6X	8X	10X	12X				
3/4 tsp	1tsp	1-1/4 tsp	1-1/2 tsp				
1-1/2 tsp	2 tsp	2-1/2 tsp	1 tbls				
1 tbls	4 tsp	5 tsp	2 tbls				
2tbls	8 tsp	10 tsp	4 tbls				
4tbls	5 tbls	7 tbls	8 tbls				
1/2 cup	1/2 cup	2/3 cup	3/4 cup				
3/4 cup	1 cup	1-1/4 cups	1-1/2 cups				
1-1/2 cups	2 cups	2-1/2 cups	3 cups				
2 cups	2-2/3 cups	3-1/3 cups	4 cups				
3 cups	4 cups	5 cups	6 cups				

Recipes for Homemade Dry Mixes

Cream of "Anything" Soup Mix

These dry mixes replace the store-bought canned versions that are so versatile in the kitchen. There are no cans to recycle and no additives or preservatives. Also, while a can of cream of chicken soup tallies up 330 calories, 23.8 fat grams, and 2,370 grams of sodium, this home version weighs in at only 95 calories, 0.2 fat grams, 710 grams of sodium, and at roughly a tenth the cost. You save in every way!

Ingredients	Quantity	X9
Nonfat dry milk powder	1/4 cup	2 cups
Cornstarch	4 teaspoons	3/4 cup
Chicken soup base	1-1/2 teaspoons	5 Tablespoons
Onion flakes	1 teaspoon	2 Tablespoons
Thyme	Dash	1 teaspoon
Dill weed	Dash	1 teaspoon
Celery salt	Dash	1 teaspoon
Yield	1/3 cup	Equivalent to 3 cups or 9 cans, 11 ounces each

Mix all ingredients and store indefinitely in a moisture-proof, airtight container at room temperature.

Use Instructions:

- 1 can cream of chicken soup = 1/3 cup dry mix, 1-1/4 cups water
- 1 can cream of mushroom soup = 1/3 cup dry mix, 1-1/4 cups water, 2 ounces finely chopped mushroom pieces, 1 teaspoon salt
- 1 can cream of celery soup = 1/3 cup dry mix, 1-1/4 cups water, 1/8 cup celery flakes or 1/2 cup chopped celery, microwaved in water until soft.

To Serve. Combine ingredients and heat until thickened, stirring constantly.

For use in casseroles: There is no need to combine the dry mix with liquid in advance, just stir it all together and cook as directed.

"Cream of Anything" Vegetarian Soup Mix

Ingredients	Quantity	X6
Vegetable soup base	3 Tablespoons	1-1/4 cups
Onion flakes	2 Tablespoons	3/4 cup
Cornstarch	1 Tablespoon	1/3 cup
Parsley flakes	2 teaspoons	1/4 cup
Yield	1/4 cup	1-1/2 cups

Combine all ingredients and store indefinitely in a moisture-proof, airtight container at room temperature.

Use Instructions:

Dry mix	1/4 cup
Milk	2 cups
Water	1 cup
Puréed cooked vegetables (choose asparagus, carrots, cauliflower, celery, broccoli, onion, peas, potatoes, spinach, corn or mushrooms)	1-1/2 cups
Yield (soup)	3 cups

Blend the dry mix into the milk and water and microwave on high until heated through, about 4-1/2 minutes. Add the puréed vegetables and heat until warm. Add salt and pepper as desired and serve hot.

Note: Purée the cooked vegetables of your choice in the blender on high for about 45 seconds. If you are blending very hot veggies, be sure to start the blender on low with the center cover removed: Hot liquids expand and may explode if closed in and turned on high.

Broth Mix

Recipes for broth from stewed chicken and other ingredients abound, and grocery stores offer 10 ounce cans for sale. This recipe provides ecology (no cans to discard), economy, no additives, no preservatives, no colorings, and terrific convenience.

Ingredients	Quantity	X6
Chicken or beef soup base	3 Tablespoons	3 cups
Cornstarch	2 teaspoons	1/3 cup
Parsley flakes	1 teaspoon	3 Tablespoons
Yield	1/3 cup	3-1/2 cups

Combine all ingredients and store indefinitely in a moisture-proof, airtight container at room temperature.

Use Instructions:

Dry mix	2 Tablespoons
Cold water	1-1/4 cups
Butter	1 teaspoon
Yield	10 ounces

Combine all ingredients and microwave on high until boiling (about 2 minutes). Stir vigorously and use as directed in recipe.

Gravy Dry Mix

This gravy mix yields 2 cups of wonderful gravy without any preservatives or food colorings—and at approximately a quarter of the price of store-bought gravy mixes and canned gravies.

Ingredients	Quantity	X12
Flour	1/3 cup	4 cups
Beef or chicken soup base	5 teaspoons	1 cup
Parsley flakes	1 Tablespoon	2/3 cup
Dried chives	2 teaspoons	1/2 cup
Thyme	1/8 teaspoon	1 teaspoon
Pepper	1/8 teaspoon	1/2 teaspoon
Yield	1/3 cup	4 cups

Combine all ingredients and store in a moisture-proof, airtight container at room temperature until needed.

Use Instructions:

Dry mix	1/3 cup	
Water	2 cups	
Yield	2 cups	

Combine the gravy mix with 1 cup of the water. Set aside. In a saucepan over medium heat, bring the other cup of water to boiling and gradually stir the gravy mixture into the water. Continue stirring until it thickens.

Note: If you combine the gravy mix with cool water and then stir constantly while adding it to the hot water, you will always have smooth, lump-free gravy.

White Sauce Mix

Keep some of this mix on hand and you will be ready to create something stunning anytime.

Ingredients	Quantity	X5
Nonfat dry milk powder	1/3 cup	1-1/2 cups
Flour	3 Tablespoons	3/4 cup
Salt	Sprinkle	1 teaspoon
Shortening (butter-flavored is best)	1 Tablespoon	1/2 cup
Yield	1/2 cup	2-1/2 cups

Combine all dry ingredients; cut in shortening. Store in moisture-proof, airtight container at room temperature for up to 6 months.

Use Instructions: Combine all ingredients for desired sauce as shown below. Cook over medium heat, stirring constantly, or in the microwave on high for 5 minutes, stirring vigorously after each 45-second interval, just until thickened.

Select One:

Thin white sauce: 1 cup water, 1/3 cup mix

Medium white sauce: 1 cup water, 1/2 cup mix

Thick white sauce: 1 cup water, 2/3 cup mix

Cheese Sauce

Make desired white sauce, add 1/4 teaspoon dry mustard, 1 cup shredded cheddar cheese.

Curry Sauce

Make desired white sauce, then add 1/4 teaspoon pepper, 1/8 teaspoon paprika, 1 teaspoon onion salt, 1 teaspoon curry powder, 1/8 teaspoon ginger, and then add 1 teaspoon lemon juice just before serving.

Béchamel

Make desired white sauce, substituting 1 cup broth (see page 60) for the cup of water. Add 1/8 teaspoon paprika to dry mix and blend all.

Mornay

Make Béchamel, then add 1/4 cup Parmesan cheese, stirring until melted and smooth.

Guacamole Seasoning Mix

This mix costs pennies per teaspoon. Compare that to the commercial mixes offered in your supermarket.

Ingredients	Quantity	X4
Sugar	1/2 teaspoon	2 teaspoons
Salt	1/4 teaspoon	1 teaspoon
Garlic powder	1/8 teaspoon	1/2 teaspoon
Cayenne	2 sprinkles	1/8 teaspoon
Yield	1 teaspoon	1/4 cup

Combine all ingredients and store indefinitely in a moisture-proof, airtight container at room temperature.

Use Instructions:

Dry mix	1 teaspoon
Avocado, mashed	1 cup
Sour cream	1/3 cup
Yield	2/3 cup

Combine all ingredients and mix well. Chill until ready to serve. If chilled for longer than a few hours, a harmless dark film will form over the surface of the dip. Simply skim it off, stir well, and serve. This guacamole keeps in refrigerator for up to 1 week.

Dill Dip Seasoning Mix

This is one of my favorite dips to take to parties, served with raw vegetables, Wheat Thins or Cheez-It® crackers.

Ingredients	Quantity	X____
Onion powder	1 teaspoon	
Dill weed	1 Tablespoon	
Spike or seasoning salt	1 teaspoon	
Yield (seasoning mix)	2 Tablespoons	

Combine and store indefinitely in a moisture-proof, airtight container at room temperature.

Use Instructions:

Seasoning mix	2 Tablespoons	
Sour cream (regular or fat-free)	1 cup	
Mayonnaise (regular or fat-free)	1 cup	
Yield	2 cups	

Combine all ingredients, mix well, and refrigerate for at least 2 hours before serving.

Taco Seasoning Mix

This dry mix is practically free but makes tacos easy, quick, and reasonable.

Ingredients	Quantity	X____
Paprika	1/4 teaspoon	
Onion flakes	2 teaspoons	
Chili powder	1 teaspoon	
Cornstarch	1/2 teaspoon	
Garlic salt	1 teaspoon	
Oregano flakes	1/4 teaspoon	
Cumin	1/2 teaspoon	
Yield	3 Tablespoons	

Mix all ingredients and store indefinitely in a moisture-proof, airtight container at room temperature.

Use Instructions:

Dry mix	1-1/2 Tablespoons
Water	1/2 cup
Ground beef	1 pound
Yield	6 servings

Stir the dry mix into the water. Brown the ground beef, then add the combined water and dry mix. Simmer for about 15 minutes, stirring occasionally. Serve with favorite taco fixings or use in any recipe calling for taco meat.

Pizza Seasoning Mix

If pizza is as popular at your house as I think it is, you will love the pizza parlor flavor this recipe affords for mere pennies.

Ingredients	Quantity	X12
Onion flakes	1/2 teaspoon	2 Tablespoons
Crushed red pepper	1/2 teaspoon	2 Tablespoons
Oregano flakes	1/4 teaspoon	1 Tablespoon
Parsley flakes	1/4 teaspoon	1 Tablespoon
Basil	1/8 teaspoon	2 teaspoons
Garlic powder	1/8 teaspoon	2 teaspoons
Salt	1/8 teaspoon	2 teaspoons
Dill weed	Sprinkle	1/2 teaspoon
Pepper	Sprinkle	1/2 teaspoon
Yield	2 teaspoons	1/2 cup

Combine all ingredients and store indefinitely in a moisture-proof, airtight container at room temperature.

Use Instructions: Use in any recipe calling for pizza seasoning mix, or combine 2 teaspoons of the mix with 8 ounces tomato sauce and assemble pizza as usual.

Spaghetti Sauce Seasoning Mix

You'll never be without spaghetti sauce again, plus you'll enjoy the convenience and taste of this recipe for a fraction of the store-bought cost.

Ingredients	Quantity	X____
Onion flakes	1 Tablespoon	
Garlic powder	1 teaspoon	
Salt	1 teaspoon	
Oregano flakes	1/4 teaspoon	
Thyme	1/4 teaspoon	
Pepper	1/8 teaspoon	
Yield	1 Tablespoon	

Combine all ingredients and store in a moisture-proof, airtight container at room temperature until needed.

Use Instructions:

Dry mix	1 Tablespoon	
Tomato sauce	15 ounces	
Olive oil	1 teaspoon	
Yield	1 Tablespoon	

Combine all ingredients in a saucepan over medium heat; bring to a boil, reduce heat, and simmer for 20 minutes or longer. Stir occasionally.

Shake-and-Bake Meat Breading Mix

This combination is easy to assemble and helps the busy cook make something special in a hurry. You won't miss paying the high price of commercial coating, either.

Ingredients	Quantity	X____
Italian Seasoning	2 teaspoons	
Dry bread crumbs	4 cups	
Celery salt	1 Tablespoon	
Garlic powder	1 teaspoon	
Paprika	1 Tablespoon	
Pepper	1 Tablespoon	
Salt	2 teaspoons	
Yield	4 cups	

Combine all ingredients and store in a moisture-proof, airtight container at room temperature for up to 6 months.

Chicken

Combine 1 cup mix with 1/2 teaspoon sage, 1/2 teaspoon thyme in a gallon-size plastic bag. Shake cut-up chicken pieces in the combination and arrange in ungreased baking dishes. Bake at 350°F for 1-1/4 hours, turning once during cooking period.

Beef or Veal

Combine 1 cup mix with 1/2 teaspoon oregano flakes in a gallon-size plastic bag. Shake individual steaks in combination and bake on greased sheets for 1 hour at 300°F.

Pork

Combine 1 cup mix with 1/4 teaspoon allspice in a gallon-size plastic bag. Shake individual chops in the mixture and bake on ungreased baking sheets at 350°F for 45 minutes.

Meat Loaf Seasoning Mix

Ingredients	Quantity	X_____
Oatmeal or bread crumbs	4 cups	
Garlic powder	1 teaspoon	
Onion flakes	1/2 cup	
Nonfat dry milk powder	3/4 cup	
Onion soup base	1/4 cup	
Oregano flakes	1 Tablespoon	
Parsley flakes	1/3 cup	
Pepper	1 teaspoon	
Yield	4-1/2 cups	

Combine all ingredients and store in a moisture-proof, airtight container at room temperature until needed.

Use Instructions:

Dry mix	1-1/2 cups
Ground beef	2 pounds
Cold water	2/3 cup
Egg, lightly beaten	1
Yield	1 meat loaf

Combine all ingredients and form into a loaf. Glaze with ketchup or other favorite topping and bake at 350°F for 1-1/4 hours. Drain fat, let stand for 10 minutes, slice, and serve.

Instant Hot Cocoa Mix

Those little envelopes from Switzerland can dent your food budget. Replace them with this excellent and domestic-priced combination.

Ingredients	Quantity	X8
Nonfat dry milk powder	1-1/3 cups	10-2/3 cups
Hershey's Chocolate Quik®	2 Tablespoons	2 cups
Powdered coffee creamer	1 Tablespoon	6 ounces
Powdered sugar	1-1/2 Tablespoons	3/4 cup
Yield	1-1/2 cups	11 cups

Combine all ingredients and store in a moisture-proof, airtight container at room temperature until needed.

Use Instructions: Measure 1/2 cup cocoa mix into 1 cup hot water. Stir, and serve.

Dried Beans Mix

Dried beans are a staple in many homes, and can be considered as a "dry mix" because they keep indefinitely in their dried state. They are a delicious, fat-free, cholesterol-free source of protein, and are much less expensive when you cook your own rather than use canned beans. If you are used to the canned variety, be aware that preparing your own beans takes several hours—and this is before they are ready to use in your favorite recipes.

The simplest, easiest way to cook beans is in an electric Crock-Pot. Just add water and beans in the ratios shown in the chart, set the Crock-Pot on High, and your beans will be ready to eat or use in recipes after 4 to 6 hours, depending on the type of bean and its age. By using a Crock-Pot, you can cook beans overnight or while you are at work—a real time-saver.

If you prefer the standard soaking method for cooking beans, place the beans in a large pot with enough water to cover them by half an inch or more. Allow beans to soak for several hours or overnight. Drain off the soaking water, then add fresh water in the ratios shown in the chart. Bring the water to a boil, then reduce heat and simmer, with the pot not quite covered, until the beans are tender but not mushy (see approximate cooking times in the chart).

Always remember to sort through and then rinse the beans before you soak them or put them in a Crock-Pot. And note that split peas and lentils do not require a presoaking; they cook very quickly.

Beans (1 cup dry)	Water	Cooking time (if presoaked)	Yield
Black beans	4 cups	1-1/2 hours	2 cups
Black-eyed peas	3 cups	1 hour	2 cups
Chickpeas (garbanzos)	4 cups	3 hours	2 cups
Cowpeas	3 cups	30 minutes	2-1/2 cups
Kidney beans	3 cups	1-1/2 hours	2 cups
Lentils and split peas (no presoaking)	3 cups	30 to 40 minutes	2-1/4 cups
Lima beans	2 cups	1-1/2 hours	1-1/4 cups
Navy beans or Great Northern beans	3-1/2 cups	2-1/4 hours	2 cups
Pinto (pink) beans	3 cups	2-1/2 hours	2 cups
Red beans	3 cups	3 hours	2 cups
Soybeans	4 cups	3 or more hours	2 cups

See also: Refried beans (page 197).

Croutons

Here's a recipe that starts in the freezer, then is made in quantity for storage at room temperature. My grandmother taught me to save any leftover bread crusts in a bag in the freezer. Then, when I wanted to make croutons for stuffing mix or to top off the perfect salad, I could make them in a flash and at no expense.

Ingredients	Quantity for cheese croutons	Quantity for regular croutons	Quantity for nonfat croutons
Bread cubes	4 cups	4 cups	4 cups
Butter, melted	6 Tablespoons	1-1/2 Tablespoons	—
Parmesan cheese	4 Tablespoons	—	—
Oregano	1/2 teaspoon	—	—
Basil	1/2 teaspoon	—	—
Garlic salt	1/4 teaspoon	—	1/4 teaspoon
Garlic powder	—	1/8 teaspoon	—
Celery salt	1/8 teaspoon	—	—
Yield	1 cup	1 cup	1 cup

Combine all ingredients and stir to coat. Spread in a baking dish and microwave on high for 3 to 5 minutes, until sizzling and browned, stirring after each minute. Croutons can also be baked at 300°F for 30 minutes, stirring after each 10 minutes. Cool completely and store in zip-top bags at room temperature for up to 6 months.

Seasoned Stuffing Mix

The original recipe equals one 6 ounce box of stuffing mix.

Ingredients	Quantity	X4
Chicken or beef soup base	1 Tablespoon	3 Tablespoons
Onion flakes	2 teaspoons	3 Tablespoons
Celery flakes	2 teaspoons	3 Tablespoons
Parsley flakes	1 teaspoon	1 Tablespoon
Thyme	1/2 teaspoon	2 teaspoons
Pepper	1/8 teaspoon	1/4 teaspoon
Salt	1/8 teaspoon	1/4 teaspoon
Yield	5 teaspoons	6 Tablespoons

Microwave bread cubes on medium high for 2 to 3 minutes, stirring after each 60-second interval, until dry. Cool completely and store in large zip-top bags, at room temperature, until needed. Combine seasonings separately and store in a small zip-top bag taped to bread cubes bag.

Use Instructions:

Dry bread crumbs	3 cups
Dry mix seasonings	5 teaspoons
Water	1/2 cup
Butter	1 Tablespoon
Yield	3 cups

Combine ingredients in a microwave-safe dish and heat on high for 2 minutes. Stir, cover, and let rest for 3 to 5 minutes; fluff up with a fork and serve.

Chapter 5

Men Pleasing Meats &
Wild Game Main Dishes

*I knew something was up the day I served a chef salad
to my new husband who looked around and said,
"Nice salad, but what's for supper?"*

Most girls love salads, pasta and sorbet, while most guys just keep asking, "Where's the beef?"

Men love meat main dishes and if you swing by my restaurant during noon rush, I can prove it. The guys are snatching up the Super Beef Soft Shells with double meat, while most of the gals are opting for Grilled Chicken or a Taco Salad.

In this chapter you will learn how to...

- serve tender, oven-baked meat entrées in 30 minutes or less,
- prepare fish and wild game like a pro,
- sauce-up your steak and meatballs for rave reviews, and
- make perfect gravy every time.

You will find all the instructions you need within each category zone. The chapter begins with a few of my own quick-fix favorites followed by meatball mania, fresh fish recipes, and wild game wisdom.

Fool-Proof Gravy

Making great gravy is easy if you know the secret. You'll enjoy smooth, lump-free gravy every time you thoroughly blend the thickener with the cold liquid before adding it to the pan drippings. The most common mistake is to add the thickener directly to the hot liquid, causing clumping.

Gravy Making Formula

$$1 + 2 + 8 = Gravy$$

1 part soup base + 2 parts thickener + 8 parts liquid

The liquid options include pan drippings, water, stock, milk, cream or some combination of these. The usual thickener is flour. If you choose cornstarch, you need to half the quantity of thickener. If you don't have any or enough pan drippings, substitutions can be found on pages 60 and 61.

I always make extra gravy because leftovers make great stew base and can also be served with meat on toast or over baked potatoes.

Chicken Fried

This is a huge favorite in the Swedberg home. Yum!

Ingredient	Quantity	X____
Venison or chicken breast filets, 1/4" thick	1 pound	
Butter	4 ounces	
Flour	1/2 cup	
Yield	4-6 servings	

Pound both sides with a meat mallet until filets are about 1/8 inch thick. Heat an ungreased electric skillet to 375°F shake filets in a zip-top bag with about 1/2 cup flour; shake off excess and set aside.

Slide 1 tablespoon butter around the bottom of skillet to coat, then quickly add a single layer of filets. Fry for 2 minutes, until slightly browned, then turn and fry until sizzly and a bit golden. Add additional butter as needed to avoid sticking. Do not overcook.

Remove to serving plate and sprinkle generously with salt and pepper. Cover filets while you finish remaining steaks. Serve hot.
Caution: Adding seasonings before frying will toughen steaks.

Chicken In a Jiffy

If you have chicken breasts thawed and company on the way, try this quick, delicious solution.

Ingredients	Quantity	X____
Butter	4 Tablespoons	
Chicken breast filets	3 to 4 pounds	
Spike or seasoning salt	1 Tablespoon	
Sliced mushrooms	2 cups fresh or 4 ounces canned	
Yield	4-6 servings	

Melt butter in bottom of a 9x13" pan. Roll filets in butter to coat; sprinkle generously with Spike. Bake with meaty side up in 450°F oven for 25 minutes. Remove pan from oven long enough to pour over the mushrooms, including liquid if canned. Return all to oven for 5 minutes. Serve with gravy made from meat drippings (see Gravy Mix on page 61).

Grilled Steak

This unexpected two-step combination of ingredients won an award in a local cooking contest when I was a child. My mom served it to us on special occasions and it has become a favorite with my children as well.

Browning Sauce

Butter	1/4 cup
Dry mustard	2 Tablespoons
Salt	2 teaspoons
Paprika	3/4 teaspoon
Cayenne	1/8 teaspoon
Honey	2 teaspoons
Yield	1/3 cup

Brown the steaks, in the browning sauce, in a skillet over medium-high heat just until coated.

Grilling Sauce

Oil	1/4 cup
Ketchup	2 Tablespoons
Honey	3/4 teaspoon
Worcestershire	2 Tablespoons
Salt	3/4 teaspoon
Yield	1/3 cup

Transfer steaks to hot grill. Baste often with the grilling sauce until cooked to desired doneness. Any remaining sauce can be stored in separate airtight containers and refrigerated for future use.

Meatball Mania

I occasionally set aside an hour to mix up a few months' worth of meatballs to freeze raw for quick meals later. Here are the recipes I love. I encourage you to try all of these, for sure, but also add your own favorite meatball recipe to your mega meat-making adventure!

Mom's Meatballs Consomme

This is from my mother's recipe collection, a memory of my childhood featuring rich flavor without the fat and without the cost of a tin can.

Ingredients	Quantity	X____
Ground beef	1 pound	
Egg, beaten	1	
Bread crumbs or oatmeal	1/2 cup	
Dry onion flakes	1 Tablespoon	
Cold water	2 cups	
Yield	18 small or 9 large meatballs	

Gravy

Beef soup base or bouillon	2 teaspoons	
Tomato paste	1/2 teaspoon	
Cornstarch	2 Tablespoons	
Yield	4-6 servings	

Combine ground beef, egg, bread crumbs, and onions; form into 1 inch meatballs. Brown and set aside. Mix remaining ingredients and pour into skillet. Heat, stirring constantly, until thickened. Add meatballs and simmer, covered, until heated through. Serve hot or keep warm in 350°F oven for up to 1 hour.

Swedish Meatballs

My mom-in-love, Doris Swedberg, shares her classic meatballs recipe for you to enjoy. I've been treated to these delicious meatballs practically every Christmas since marrying into this Swedish family.

Ingredients	Quantity	X____
Ground Beef	1 pound	
Ground Pork	1/2 pound	
Minced Onion	1/2 cup	
Dry Onion Flakes	1 Tablespoon	
Egg	1	
Parsley	1 Tablespoon	
Salt	2 teaspoons	
Worcestershire	1 teaspoon	
Pepper	1/8 teaspoon	
Yield	24 small or 12 large meatballs	

Mix thoroughly, cover and refrigerate at least 2 hours. Shape into balls and brown slowly, cooking until done. Remove meatballs from pan.

Gravy

Ingredients	Quantity
Water	2 cups, divided
Flour	1/4 cup
Paprika	1 teaspoon
Salt	1/2 teaspoon
Pepper	1/8 teaspoon
Sour cream	1/2 - 3/4 cup

Over medium heat, stir 1 cup water into pan drippings. Combine remaining water with flour and seasonings. Whisk together until smooth, then gradually whisk into the boiling mixture. Boil one minute. Reduce heat to low and stir in the sour cream. Add the meatballs and heat through.

Big Batch BBQ Meatballs

I usually make up one batch of these in early November, as these meatballs are a huge hit at parties.

Ingredients	Quantity	X4
Ground beef	1 pound	4 pounds
Sausage	1/2 pound	2 pounds
Eggs	1	4
Oatmeal	1 cup	4 cups
Water	1/4 cup	1 cup
Powdered milk	3 Tablespoons	2/3 cup
Chili powder	1 Tablespoon	1/4 cup
Onion Flakes	1 Tablespoon	1/4 cup
Pepper	1 teaspoon	1 Tablespoon
Garlic powder	1 teaspoon	1 Tablespoon
Yield	3 dozen small or 18 large meatballs	4-8 dozen meatballs

To Freeze: Mix well and form meatballs. Set close together, but not touching, on cookie sheets. Freeze until firm, then slide into clean ice cream buckets or zip top containers until needed.

BBQ Sauce of Meatballs

Ketchup	1 cup	4 cups
Brown sugar	3/4 cup	3 cups
Liquid smoke	2 teaspoons	2 Tablespoons
Garlic powder	1 teaspoon	1 Tablespoon
Onion flakes	1 teaspoon	1 Tablespoon

Mix well and store in refrigerator. Pour 1/2 cup sauce per dozen meatballs over top and bake, covered, at 350°F, 60 minutes from frozen, 35 for thawed.

Fresh Fish

Whether you opt to deep fry or pan fry your fillets, I encourage you to serve them with the best Tarter Sauce ever. The recipe is on page 210.

Pan Fried Fish

Incredients	Quantities	X____
Fillets	1 pound	
Egg	1	
Biscuit Mix (recipe page 162)	1/4 cup	
Oil	2 Tablespoons	
Favorite seasonings	Dash	
Yield	4-6 servings	

Preheat skillet to 375°F. Add oil. Dip each fillets in egg then flour. Pan fry 2-3 minutes until meat begins to loose its glossy sheen. Flip and fry until golden brown. Sprinkle with seasonings like salt and lemon pepper.

Deep Fried Fish

Ingredients	Quantity	X____
Flour	Enough to coat fillets	
Flour	1-1/2 cups	
Salt	1 teaspoon	
Lukewarm water	1-1/2 cups	
Oil	6 Tablespoons	
Fish fillets	2-4 pounds	
Egg whites	2	
Yield	4-6 servings	

Sift together the flour and salt. In a separate bowl combine water and oil. Gently blend in flour combination and let stand at room temperature for 2 hours* or longer. Dredge fillets in flour,** shaking off excess. Heat oil in deep fat fryer to 425°F. Beat egg whites just until they hold their shape: do not overbeat. Gently fold egg whites into room temperature batter. Dip each floured fillets into batter and then into hot oil. Fry until golden on both sides, turning if needed. Remove to paper toweling and sprinkle with salt.

---

*2 hours is the ideal time for the batter to rest because a fermentation process offers a softer coating. Waiting 20 minutes to 4 hours will yield satisfactory results.

**Use plain flour because seasoning the fillets at this point toughens them.

***Fry as many fillets at a time as you wish, using a metal spatula to keep them submerged. The batter does not stick of crumble so you can fry many, many fillets at once.

Wild Game Wisdom

The following wild game recipes are a gift to you from my sister-in-love, Lynnette Danielson. Lynnette is a pro at cooking venison, duck, goose, pheasant, and more. As the mother of five boys, living in "The Land of the Giants," (as my dad always called the Danielson residence), she fed these growing men, all of whom are now six feet three inches and taller. As they grew, they hunted, and they ate their game. Through the preparation of thousands of wild game dinners, for family and friends, Lynnette perfected some awesome recipes she has gifted to us here. Enjoy!

Lynnette's Rules for Wild Game

1. Biggest problem is over-cooking. Contrary to popular belief, you should not cook it to death!
2. Irrigate pellet holes to remove feathers and blood from game birds.
3. Freshly cleaned game lasts up to one week in the refrigerator.
4. Tomatoes accentuate the wild flavor of game.

The Danielson Men

From left to right: Eric, Joel, Jedd, Michael, Gary & Nathan Danielson

Swiss

Ingredients	Quantity	X____
Venison or beef steaks	1 pound	
Onions	1 large	
Celery	1 medium stalk	
Tomatoes, canned	1 cup	
Worcestershire sauce	2 Tablespoons	
Salt	Dash	
Pepper	Dash	
Canola oil	2 Tablespoons	
Yield	4-6 servings	

Steaks should be about 1 inch thick. Dredge with flour and season with salt and pepper, then brown in hot oil. Combine remaining ingredients and pour over browned steaks. Cover tightly and cook in medium oven (350°F) for 60 minutes, or in crock pot on high 3-4 hours or low 6-8 hours. Remove meat to hot holding platter and make gravy from drippings in the pan.

Variation: Substitute one envelop dry onion soup mix, and 1-10 ounces can cream of mushroom soup for the onion, celery, tomatoes, and Worcestershire sauce.

Stir Fry

Ingredients	Quantity	X____
Pheasant or beef breast filets, or venison steaks, 1/4" thick	1 pound	
Soy Sauce	2 Tablespoons	
Ginger	1/2 teaspoon	
Garlic	2 cloves	
Canola oil	3 Tablespoons, divided	
Broccoli florets	2 cups	
Cauliflower, sliced	1 cup	
Carrot, thinly slice	1 cup	
Water	3/4 cup	
Soy sauce	1/4 cup	
Cornstarch	4 teaspoons	
Yield	4-6 servings	

Mix together soy sauce, ginger, and garlic. Add meat pieces and marinate 10 minutes. In a large skillet or wok, heat 2 tablespoons oil over medium high heat, add marinated meat and stir-fry about 5-7 minutes. Remove meat and set aside, add remaining tablespoon of oil to skillet and add vegetables. Stir fry to desired tenderness, add cooked meat. Combine last 3 ingredients for sauce. Stir into hot meat/vegetables before serving. Serve over rice.

Shish Kabob Marinade

Ingredients	Quantity	X____
Chicken breast filets or venison, beef or pork steaks or chops, cubed	1 pound	
Oil	1/4 cup	
Soy sauce	1/4 cup	
Ketchup	3-4 Tablespoons	
Vinegar	2 Tablespoons	
Garlic powder	Sprinkle	
Yield	4-6 servings	

Mix all ingredients. Add meat. Marinate at least 4 hours before cooking. Skewer cubed meat. Grill 3-4 minutes per side. Grill whole filets until done. Use a thermometer so you don't overcook.

Parmigiano

Ingredients	Quantity	X____
Wild/store-bought turkey, pheasant or chicken breast filets, or venison or beef steaks	1 pound	
Eggs, beaten	2	
Salt	3/4 teaspoon	
Pepper	1/8 teaspoon	
Fine bread crumbs	1 cup	
Parmesan Cheese, grated	1/2 cup	
Butter	1/3 cup	
Pasta sauce	26 ounces	
Oregano	1 teaspoon	
Onion salt	1/4 teaspoon	
Yield	4-6 servings	

Dip filets in egg, and then in a mixture of the next 4 ingredients. Brown on both sides in a skillet with melted butter.

In a 9x13" pan, combine the spaghetti sauce, oregano, and onion salt. Place browned meat into the sauce. Top each piece with a slice of Mozzarella cheese. Bake 20-30 at 350°F. Serve with spaghetti noodles.

Alfredo Alternative

Substitute Alfredo sauce for the pasta sauce and eliminate the oregano and onion.

Creamed

Ingredients	Quantity	X____
Pheasant or chicken breast filets, or venison or beef steaks	1 pound	
Soy sauce	2 Tablespoons	
Ginger	1/2 teaspoon	
Minced garlic	1/2 teaspoon	
Butter	2 Tablespoons	
Onion, chopped	1 small	
Mushrooms, chopped, save liquid	4 ounces	
Cream of chicken or Mushroom soup	10 ounces	
Parmesan cheese, grated	1/2 cup	
Chicken broth	1 cup	
Flour	2 Tablespoons	
Yield	4-6 servings	

Slice meat diagonally to 1/4" thickness and marinate at least 10 minutes in soy sauce, ginger, and garlic. Saute in butter. When cooked through, add onion and mushrooms and sauté until tender.

Mix together creamed soup, Parmesan cheese, chicken broth, saved mushroom liquid and flour. Add to meat. Cook on medium-low heat till bubbly and thickened. Serve over cooked noodles.

Glazed

Ingredients	Quantity	X____
Pheasant or chicken breast filets, venison or beef steaks, 1/2" thick	1 pound	
Butter	5 Tablespoons	
Garlic, minced	2 cloves	
Mushrooms, fresh or canned, drained and sliced	4 ounces	
Apple juice	1/4 cup	
Green onions, chopped	3	
Yield	4-6 servings	

In a skillet, melt 2 tablespoons butter. Cook the steaks for 3-5 minutes per side. Remove from pan and keep warm. Add rest of butter to pan, lower heat and sauté the garlic and mushrooms till tender. Add the apple juice and green onions to the mushrooms and return steaks to pan. Cook until sauce is hot again.

Stew

Ingredients	Quantity	X____
Venison, beef, duck or goose stew meat	2 pounds	
Carrots, 1" slices	2 cups	
Celery, 1" slices	2 cups	
Potatoes, 1" cubes	2 cups	
Onion chopped	1 medium	
Salt	1 teaspoon	
Pepper	1/4 teaspoon	
Beef broth	14-1/2 ounce can	
Canned tomatoes, optional	1 pint	
Canola oil	2 Tablespoons	
Yield	4-6 servings	

In a dutch oven, brown cubes of meat in hot oil just until brown. Add carrots, celery, potatoes, and onions. Add beef broth, seasonings, and tomatoes, if desired. Bring to boil, turn down heat and simmer 2 hours or place in crockpot on low all day.

Grilled Game Birds

Ingredients	Quantity	X____
Wild/store-bought turkey, pheasant or chicken breast filets	1 pound	
Soy sauce	1/4 cup	
Cooking oil	1/4 cup	
Orange juice or ketchup	1/4 cup	
Minced dry onion or garlic	2 Tablespoons	
Lemon juice or vinegar	2 Tablespoons	
Ground ginger	1/4 teaspoon	
Garlic salt	dash	
Pepper	dash	
Yield	4-6 servings	

Combine all ingredients except filets in shallow dish; mix well. Reserve two tablespoons of marinade. Rinse and pat filets dry. Add to remaining marinade, turn to coat.

Marinate, covered, in refrigerator for several hours or 30 minutes at room temperature, turning occasionally; drain.

Grill on both sides until thermometer reads 160°F, basting once or twice with reserved marinade.

Grilled Duck

Ingredients	Quantity	X____
Wild duck filets	1 pound	
Bacon, precooked	1/2 pound	
Zesty Italian Dressing	1 cup	
Lawry's Seasoning Salt	To rub	
Yield	4-6 servings	

Slice breasts crosswise, 1-1/2" thick. Tenderize by hammering breasts to 3/4" and marinate 24 hours in the Zesty Italian Dressing, reserving 2 tablespoons for basting. Refrigerate at least 24 hours. Wrap meat in pre-cooked bacon with a toothpick to hold it together. Dust with Lawry's Seasoning Salt as you place it on hot grill to sear in juices. Grill until thermometer reads 160°F. Do not overcook.

Michael Danielson is a recent Business Administration graduate. As Lynnette's youngest son, he shared the above rendition which he perfected through years of cooking hundreds of ducks.

When I told him how impressed I was, he replied, "I was possessed to find a way to eat the ducks without actually tasting the ducks!"

Chapter 6

International Cuisine

Take your friends on
a taste-trip around the world
with these easy and delicious
Italian, Chinese & Mexican favorites.

Have you ever imagined owning your own Mexican or Italian restaurant? I never had, but now I do. I can tell you, it's a lot of work and a lot of fun! About the only thing I wish we could add to our menu is Chinese cuisine, just because I love it so much.

If you aren't prepared to open up your own shop, why not turn your home into a restaurant every now and again?

When I wrote the first version of this book, entertaining guests for meals was very common in America. People did it all the time. Now, it's quite an honor to receive a meal invitation to dine in someone's home.

But dining in is still viable: It's personal, it's honoring and it's far less expensive than eating out, especially at fancy restaurants.

While the average fast food restaurant marks up its prices two to three times, a sit-down restaurant requires a higher margin. Even an ice cream shop can run a mark-up of four to five times the cost of the ingredients.

Many of the times we opt for eating out with friends, it's because we feel we don't have time to both clean the house *and* cook a meal.

But if you want to host a dinner, and only have enough time to prepare the house, why not invite friends or extended family for a shared meal where everyone contributes a prepared meal component? At least one-third of the entertaining I do in my home is in this fashion.

Shared or Bring-Your-Own (BYO) events work great for brunches, dinners, dessert buffets and almost any kind of party. The host bakes or offers a few special dishes, arranges a buffet table with room for everyone's contributions and focuses her attention on preparing the home. Cooperative parties like this are fun, can be thrown at the last minute (well, within the last 24 hours), and provide a unique opportunity to taste everyone else's favorite dishes.

Besides, we have found that people feel better about showing up for a meal if they can bring something to share. Food is both a practical and delicious solution—freeing up the host's time and budget to do it more often.

One of my favorite parties to host revolves around International cuisine and the recipes in this section will make you look like a pro, whether you make all the dinner components yourself or invite your guests to bring some of the evenings' edible fare.

Here are a few sample invitations for hosting a BYO party:

- **Trip Around the World.** Enjoy International cuisine of all sorts on [Day, Date] from [Start-Finish Time] at [Location]. Bring any entrée, side or dessert from the ethnic food genre of your choice. Passports and beverages provided. Be sure to bring along a copy of your recipe!
- **Chinese Potluck.** Join friends at [Location] on [Day, Date] from [Start-Finish Time] for a shared meal featuring Chinese cuisine. Bring your favorite homemade or take-out entrée or side dish, or bring a chocolate dessert of any kind. Chopsticks and beverages provided. Be sure to bring along a copy of your recipe!
- **Italian Pizza & Bruschetta.** Bring your favorite pizza ingredients to

[Location] on [Day, Date] at [Start Time]. We'll provide the Bruschetta and beverages.

- **Mexican Taco Feed.** We'll provide the shells, meat, and Fried Ice Cream Dessert. Wear a sombrero and bring your favorite taco toppings plus a beverage. Party begins at [Start Time] on [Day, Date] at [Location].

When hosting an International party, one of your responsibilities is to decorate the table. Create a centerpiece using a world globe or similarly eye-catching focal point. Use your own or borrowed memorabilia from well-traveled friends, combined with disposable or your most-appropriate dishes, silverware and glasses. Bandanas make fun napkins for Mexican parties, and so on. Display tips are found in chapter 9.

Again, if you don't find the taste you crave in this section, search Google and you'll have great options at your fingertips within seconds. My site, www.IdeasforWomensMinistry.com, includes over 30 party invitations that are ready to personalize and print, including "Trip Around the World" and others. There is a small monthly membership fee, but for that fee you also get access to all of my online resources. Check it out!

To make the components for a Mexican party yourself, begin your fiesta with the excellent Sopaipilla recipe on page 51, then make Burritos or Chimichangas (page 104) plus a terrific Mexican dessert (page 103). Serve nacho chips topped with jalapeno peppers, black olives, and a generous sprinkle of shredded cheddar cheese, micro-waved on high for 90 seconds. Display surrounded with bowls of lettuce, tomato, guacamole (page 63), and salsa (page 106).

If Mexican is too spicy, Chinese is an excellent option. I used to treat myself by driving halfway across Minneapolis to pay premium for a side order of four small pieces of Shrimp Toast. Since I couldn't buy them now if I wanted to (since I live 365 miles away and no one here sells them), I came up with my own version (page 107) that costs a few cents each. You can turn your kitchen into a Chinese restaurant anytime you like. Finding additional Chinese recipes is as easy as doing a simple Google search.

Then, of course, there is always the popular and delicious Italian. The first two recipes in this section come from my sailboat-dwelling, hostess-extraordinaire, baby sister, Vicki Foster. They are fast, easy and taste exactly like the expensive restaurant versions.

Italian Cheese Loaf

Cut an 11" loaf of Italian bread in half as for a sandwich. Smother top and bottom halves with Italian Butter (recipe follows). Top liberally with Mozzarella cheese and sprinkle with oregano, and Parmesan. Place on a baking sheet, and broil until cheese is slightly browned and bubbly. Slice and serve.

Italian Butter

Ingredients	Quantity	X____
Butter, room temperature	1/4 pound	
Garlic powder	2 teaspoons	
Onion salt	1 teaspoon	
Parsley flakes	1 teaspoon	
Yield	8 Tablespoons	

Whip all ingredients together.

Italian Buttered Bread Strips   No Italian bread in the house? Toast slices of regular bread in toaster, smother with Italian Butter, and broil with buttered sides up, for 2 minutes or until sizzling. Slice into strips and serve hot.

Bruschetta

Feel free to replace the Mozzarella with Parmesan in this rich Italian pizza, but not vise versa. The unique taste relies heavily on the flavor of the Parmesan.

Ingredients	Quantity	X____
Pizza Crust	1 large or 4 small	
Mozzarella, shredded	1 cup	
Roma tomatoes	4	
Mayonnaise	1 cup	
Parmesan, shredded	1/4 cup	
Basil, fresh or squeezed	1 Tablespoon	
Garlic	1 clove	
Yield	1 large or 4 small	

Arrange the Mozzarella and finely sliced tomatoes atop the crust. Combine remaining ingredients and spoon over until well-covered. Cook at 375°F for 20 minutes or until bubbly. Slice and serve.

Note: For a completely different look but the same great taste, invert the process by putting the cheese combo directly on the crust, topped with the sliced tomatoes and Mozzarella.

Pesto

This authentic Italian taste goes together quickly and costs only a fraction of the specialty shop variety.

Ingredients	Quantity	X___
Olive oil	1/2 cup	
Parmesan	1/3 cup	
Chopped walnuts	2 Tablespoons	
Garlic powder	1 Tablespoon	
Basil	1 teaspoon	
Parsley flakes	1 teaspoon	
Yield	2/3 cup	

Combine ingredients in a blender and whir until smooth. Serve over spaghetti or pour into a glass jar and cover with a thin layer of olive oil. When ready to use, pour off the oil, and measure our needed amount (usually 2 to 3 tablespoons per recipe). Cover remaining pesto with same oil and return to the refrigerator for up to 8 months or freeze for up to 1 year. If you freeze pesto in ice cube trays, it's easy to snap out a single portion whenever you need it.

Deep-Dish Pizza Dough

In our supermarket, a pre-packaged, deep-dish pizza dough without any toppings sells for ten times the cost of this quick-and-easy recipe.

Ingredients	Quantity	Do not expand
Yeast	1 Tablespoon	
Flour	2-1/2 cups	
Sugar	1 teaspoon	
Salt	1 teaspoon	
105–115°F water	3/4 cup	
Oil	2 Tablespoons	
Yield	12" pizza	

Mix dry ingredients together with a fork; add water and oil all at once, stirring only until dough forms (do not worry if a bit of flour remains in bowl). Let rest at room temperature for 5 minutes. Spread dough onto a greased pizza pan and top with 8 ounces pizza sauce plus additional toppings as desired. Freeze for future use or bake for 20 minutes at 425°F, or until cheese is melted and bubbly.
Note: To make additional deep-dish pizza crust, measure individual recipes out into separate bowls.

Italian Lasagna

This dish is easy, affordable, and low in fat if you opt for nonfat cheeses.

Ingredients	Quantity	X____
Ground beef, browned	1 pound	
Spaghetti Sauce Seasoning Mix (page 67)	1 package (2 Tablespoons)	
Tomato sauce	30 ounces	
Cottage cheese	16 ounces	
Lasagna noodles, uncooked	8 ounces	
Parmesan cheese	1/2 cup	
Mozzarella cheese	8 ounces	
Cheddar cheese	4 ounces	
Yield	9x13" pan.	

Combine cooked ground beef, spice mix, and tomato sauce. Spread 1 cup of this combination in an ungreased baking dish. Layer a third of the noodles, Parmesan cheese, and Mozzarella cheese, then repeat, starting again with beef mixture, until all are used up. Pour 1/2 cup water around sides of pan and cover tightly with aluminum foil. Freeze for later, or bake for 1 hour at 350°F, sprinkle with cheddar cheese, and let stand for 20 minutes. Just before serving, place under broiler until cheese is bubbly.

From Frozen: Place tightly covered pan (still frozen) in cold oven. Turn the oven to 350°F and let lasagna bake for 90 minutes. Remove to counter and sprinkle with cheddar cheese. Let stand for 20 minutes, then place under broiler until cheese is bubbly.

Fried Ice Cream Dessert—Mexican Style

Ingredients	Quantity	X____
Butter, melted	6 Tablespoons	12 Tablespoons
Brown sugar	3/4 cup	1-1/2 cups
Corn flakes, crushed	2 cups	4 cups
Coconut	1/3 cup	2/3 cup
Walnuts, chopped	1/3 cup	2/3 cup
Vanilla ice cream	4 cups	1/2 gallon
Yield	8x8" pan	9x13" pan

Combine the butter and brown sugar; mix in the corn flakes, coconut, and walnuts. Layer most of the crumb mixture on the bottom of pan. Spread ice cream evenly over top and sprinkle with remaining crumbs. Freeze. When ready to serve, cut into squares.

Optional: Drizzle hot fudge sauce over top.

Burritos/Chimichangas

Once you know how to make burritos, it's easy to make chimi-changas, which are essentially fried burritos.

Burrito/Chimichanga Dry Seasoning Mix

Ingredients	Quantity	X____
Onion flakes	2 Tablespoons	
Oregano flakes	1 teaspoon	
Ground cumin	1/4 teaspoon	
Garlic powder	1/8 teaspoon	
Yield	2 Tablespoons	

Combine dry ingredients and store in moisture-proof, airtight container at room temperature until needed. Use following instructions or add 1 tablespoon vinegar and use as a replacement for prepackaged store-bought chimichanga seasoning mix.

Burrito/Chimichanga Filling

Dry mix	2 Tablespoons	
Ground beef, browned	1 cup	
Tomato sauce	1 cup	
Water	1 Tablespoon	
White vinegar	1 Tablespoon	
Yield	2 cups	

Simmer ingredients for 15 to 20 minutes, stirring occasionally, until almost all of the moisture evaporates. Remove from heat and cool slightly or store in an airtight container in the fridge or freezer until needed.

Burritos

Filling mix	2 cups
Corn or flour tortillas	8 - 8" shells
Shredded cheddar cheese	1 cup
Yield	8 burritos

Place tortillas shell on a microwave-safe dish, cover tightly with plastic wrap, and microwave on high for one minute. Remove the plastic and measure 1/4 cup hot filling into the center of each tortilla and fold like an envelope. Cool and freeze for future use, or garnish with cheddar cheese and other favorites such as sour cream, guacamole, shredded lettuce, or diced tomatoes, and serve hot.

Chimichangas

Filling mix	2 cups
Corn or flour tortillas	8 - 8" shells
Oil for frying	
Yield	8 chimichangas

Heat 1 inch of oil in skillet to 350°F. Measure 1/4 cup filling into center of each tortilla, then fold like an envelope, securing with toothpicks. Fry for about 2 minutes, turn, and continue frying until golden brown. Remove to paper towels to drain. Cool and freeze or garnish as desired and serve hot.

From Frozen: Place frozen chimichangas or burritos on a cookie sheet and lay a piece of aluminum foil loosely over top (to prevent overbrowning). Heat in 375°F oven for 20 to 25 minutes

Salsa

If you garden, this combination is pretty much free. If not, you will still come out far ahead of the regular price for the store bought version, while saving the earth yet another glass jar.

Ingredients	Quantity	X____
Green pepper	1	
Jalapeno peppers	2	
Onion	1-2	
Medium tomatoes	4	
Garlic powder	1/2 teaspoon	
Salt	1/2 teaspoon	
Lemon juice	2 Tablespoons	
Yield	4 cups	

Finely dice peppers and onion. Peel the tomatoes and whir on high in a blender for 30 seconds. Combine all ingredients and stir (do not use blender). Store in an airtight container in refrigerator for up to 3 weeks or preserve in jars according to standard preserving guidelines.

Shrimp Toast

Ingredients	Quantity	X____
Oil for frying		
Flour	1/2 cup	
Cornstarch	2 Tablespoons	
Salt	1 teaspoon	
Sugar	1/2 teaspoon	
Ginger	1/4 teaspoon	
Egg	1	
Oil	1 teaspoon	
Water	1/2 cup	
Tiny peeled shrimp	1 4 ounce can	
White bread	10 slices	
Yield	40 triangles	

Heat 2 inches of oil to 375°F. Combine dry ingredients, set aside. Combine egg, 1 teaspoon oil, water, and shrimp; stir well and then mix with dry ingredients. Slice each piece of bread into 4 equal triangles.

Place one bread triangle onto a metal spatula that you are holding in your good hand (right hand for right-handed people, etc.). Use your other hand to spoon some of the shrimp mixture onto the triangle, then immediately and carefully submerge it in the hot oil. Slip the spatula out from under the bread and repeat with additional triangles until first toast is ready to turn (it will be golden brown underneath and ready in less than 3 minutes). Turn it over and allow it to brown on the second side. Remove to a cooling rack that is covered with paper towels. Let drain while you fry the remaining toasts. Serve immediately or keep warm at 250°F for up to 45 minutes (door slightly ajar).

These freeze well and can be reheated in the oven from frozen. Place desired number on ungreased baking sheet and lay a piece of aluminum foil loosely over top. Bake at 400°F for 10 to 12 minutes until heated through.

Egg Rolls

Ingredients	Quantity	X____
Ground pork	1 pound	
Salt	1/2 teaspoon	
Cornstarch	1/2 teaspoon	
Soy sauce	1/2 teaspoon	
Green cabbage, finely shredded	1 head (approximately 2-1/2 pounds)	
Oil	2 Tablespoons	
Salt	1 teaspoon	
Five-spice powder	1 teaspoon	
Egg roll wrappers	1 pound	
Oil for frying		
Yield	24 egg rolls	

Combine pork, salt, cornstarch, and soy sauce; cover and refrigerate for 20 minutes. While waiting, blanch the cabbage in boiling water for 2 minutes. Rinse immediately in cold water and drain well. Squeeze off for excess liquid. Stir-fry pork combination in 2 tablespoons oil until no longer pink. Add cabbage, salt, and 5-spice powder; mix then cool. Roll 1/2 cup filling into each egg roll wrapper as shown in the illustration on the next page. Heat 2 inches of oil to 370°F and fry egg rolls, seam side down, until golden; turn and let fry until golden. Remove to paper-towel-covered cooling racks. Cool and freeze, or serve hot with soy sauce or Sweet 'N' Sour Sauce (page 112).

From Frozen: Place frozen rolls on an ungreased baking sheet and lay a piece of aluminum foil loosely over top. Bake in 350°F oven for 20 minutes or until heated through.

FOLDING EGG ROLLS

Note: Egg roll wrappers should be kept covered with a damp towel.

1. Place cup filling just below the center of the egg roll wrapper.
2. Fold up the bottom edge.
3. Bring in the two outside corners.
4. Complete the "envelope" by dabbing water on the fourth corner before rolling the egg roll closed.

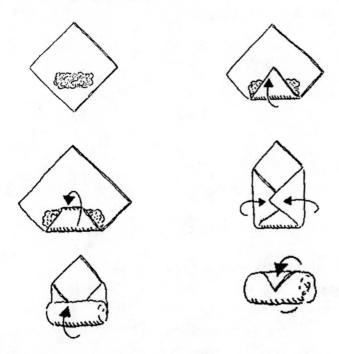

Chow Mein

Fast, easy, inexpensive, low-fat, and delicious.

Ingredients	Quantity	X____
Onion, diced	1/2 cup	
Celery, chopped	2 cups	
Water	1-1/2 cups	
Chop suey vegetables or soybeans	14 ounce can	
Meat, cooked and cut up (leftover or stir-fried beef, chicken, or turkey)	1 cup	
Cornstarch	2 Tablespoons	
Cold water	2 Tablespoons	
Soy sauce	1 Tablespoon	
Sugar	1 teaspoon	
Yield	4 servings	

Combine onion, celery, and water in a large saucepan; bring to a boil, reduce heat, and simmer for 10 minutes. Add vegetables and meat; cover and simmer for 5 minutes. In a small bowl, mix the cornstarch, cold water, soy sauce, and sugar. Pour into vegetable mixture, stirring constantly until thickened (about 2 minutes). Serve immediately over rice or let simmer, stirring occasionally, until ready to serve.

Fried Rice

Ingredients	Quantity	X____
Uncooked rice	2/3 cup	
Onion, chopped	1 medium	
Celery, chopped	2 stalks	
Oil	2 Tablespoons	
Boiling water	1-1/2 cups	
Beef or chicken soup base	1 Tablespoon	
Soy sauce	2 Tablespoons	
Cooked pork, chicken, or tiny shrimp, diced	1-1/2 cups	
Yield	4 servings	

Cook and stir rice, onion, and celery in hot oil until rice is golden brown and onion is tender. Stir in remaining ingredients; heat to boiling. Lower heat, cover tightly, and simmer for 15 minutes without removing lid. Remove from heat and fluff with a fork. Cover and let stand for an additional 10 minutes. Serve hot.

Sweet 'N Sour Sauce

You can pay the price for Chinese takeout, pay the price for the
jarred variety at your local market, or make it yourself for under a
buck.

Ingredients	Quantity	X____
Pineapple juice	1/2 cup	
Ketchup	1/2 cup	
Honey	3 Tablespoons	
Water	2 Tablespoons	
Vinegar	1 Tablespoon	
Cornstarch	4 teaspoons	
Mustard	1 teaspoon	
Salt	1/4 teaspoon	
Yield	1 cup	

Combine all ingredients in a microwave-safe dish, stir well and
cook on high, stirring every 30 seconds, until thick and smooth.

Chapter 7

Meals on Wheels

A sure way to assist a new mom,
an elderly shut-in, a sick relative,
or a friend returning from an extended
trip is to take them a home cooked meal.

This section was perfected over the 10 years I hosted a girls club in my home on Elk Street in the small town of Warroad, Minnesota. Two or three afternoons each week, about 15 minutes after school was dismissed, a public school bus would pull up in front of my house and deposit two to fifteen girls on my doorstep. While many in my community came to know us as "The Amah-El Club," the group to call when someone needed a meal, the bus drivers playfully labeled us, "The Girls on Elk Street."

As we worked together in my home kitchen, the girls learned how to cook and I learned patience (along with some useful tips that I can now share with you about making wonderful meals on wheels).

If you want to hear the rest of the story about "The Girls on Elk Street," or how to start your own cooking club, order a copy of my 200-page eBook, "Girls, Games & Gifts of Encouragement" from www.Marnie.com.

My purpose here is to help you think through the differences between an oven-to-table meal and one that is going to be delivered. In this chapter I provide several meal ideas that hold their temperature well and get rave reviews.

You'll notice that the instructions in this section are formatted differently from those in the rest of the book. When teaching children how to cook, it is best to use numbered lists and to add cooking tips within the recipes.

One other piece of advice: When preparing food to go, send the meals in disposable containers as the recipient may not have the energy to do much clean-up. Also, disposable dishes never break or chip, and they will feel no pressure to return dishes to you in a timely manner. The family can just relax and enjoy the meal.

Layered Lettuce Salad

In the end, this was the only lettuce salad I would send out. It holds its temperature and flavor well, it is as good on day one as day three and it always gets rave reviews.

	Small Quantity	X2	X4
Lettuce, shredded	1/2 head	1 head 2 heads	
Onion, chopped	1/4 cup	1/2 cup	1 cup
Celery, chopped	1/4 cup	1/2 cup	1 cup
Peas, frozen	1/2 cup	1 cup	2 cups
Miracle Whip	1 cup	2 cups	4 cups
Sugar	1 Tablespoon	2 Tablespoon	1/4 cup
Bacon slices, cooked, drained and crumbled	3 slices	6 slices	12 slices
Cheddar cheese, shredded	1/4 cup	1/2 cup	1 cup
Yield	8x8" pan	9x13" pans	2-9x13" pans

1. Cook the bacon over low heat, turning often.
2. When cooked, drain between paper towels. Set aside.
3. Shred the lettuce and place it on the bottom. (This is a layered salad: DO NOT MIX the ingredients!)
4. Chop the onion and place the correct amount over the lettuce.
5. Chop the celery and layer atop the onion.
6. Measure the frozen peas and add them. (Remember, DO NOT MIX.)
7. In a different bowl, stir together the Miracle Whip and sugar.
8. Spread this mixture evenly over the peas. (The goal is to seal the salad ingredients underneath the Miracle Whip mixture so no air can get in.)
9. Crumble the cooled bacon pieces over the salad.
10. Sprinkle the cheese over the bacon.
11. Cover tightly.
12. Label the container.
13. Refrigerate for up to five days. (As long as there are no salad ingredients breaking the Miracle Whip seal, this salad will be as good on the 4th or 5th day as it is on the first.)

Main Dishes To Go

Chicken Tortilla

	Quantity	X2	X4
Chicken, cooked and diced	1 cup	2 cups	4 cups
Flour tortillas, 8"	6	12	24
Cream of chicken soup	1 can	2 cans	4 cans
Chicken broth	1/4 cup	1/2 cup	1 cup
Salsa	1/2 cup	1 cup	2 cups
Onions, finely diced	1/4 cup	1/2 cup	1 cup
Olives, sliced	1/4 cup	1/2 cup	1 cup
Cheddar cheese	3/4 cup	1-1/2 cups	3 cups
Yield	8" pie plate or 8x8" pan	2 pie plates or a 9x13" pan	4 pie plates or 2-9x13" pans

1. Preheat the oven to 350°F.
2. Tear tortillas into 1" pieces.
3. Finely chop the onions.
4. Combine all ingredients except the cheese.
5. Scoop 1/3 of the mixture into bottom of the pan(s). Layer over 1/3 of the cheese. Repeat to make three layers.
6. Cover with tin foil and bake for 45 minutes.

Wild Rice Casserole

	Quantity	X2	X3
Ground beef, browned, drained	2 cups	4 cups	6 cups
Celery, chopped small	2 cups	4 cups	6 cups
Wild rice, cooked ahead	2 cups	4 cups	6 cups
White rice, cooked ahead	2 cups	4 cups	6 cups
Mushroom pieces with liquid	6 ounces can	12 ounces	18 ounces
Soy sauce	1/3 cup	2/3 cup	1 cup
Onion powder	1 teaspoon	2 teaspoons	1 Tablespoon
Accent	1 teaspoon	2 teaspoons	1 Tablespoon
Chicken bouillon	2 teaspoons	4 teaspoons	2 Tablespoons
Thyme	1 teaspoon	2 teaspoons	1 Tablespoon
Parsley flakes	1 teaspoon	2 teaspoons	1 Tablespoon
Yield	2 pie plates or a 9x13" pan	4 pie plates or 2-9x13" pans	6 pie plates or 3-9x13" pans

1. Preheat the oven to 350°F.
2. Brown the hamburger; drain.
3. Chop the celery.
4. Combine the burger, celery, and rice in a large bowl.
5. Add the mushrooms, reserving the liquid.
6. In a separate bowl, combine the mushroom juice, soy sauce and remaining ingredients.
7. Stir well then pour over the rice combination.
8. Stir to blend.
9. Scoop into pans.
10. Bake 9x13's for thirty minutes and pie plates or casseroles for 20 minutes.

Glazed Ham Slices

Consider using turkey ham: it tastes great and is substantially less expensive in both cost and fat grams.

	4-5 servings	8-10 servings
Brown sugar	1/2 cup	1 cup
Flour	1 Tablespoon	2 Tablespoons
Dry mustard	1/2 teaspoon	1 teaspoon
Cinnamon	1/4 teaspoon	1/2 teaspoon
Water	1 Tablespoon	2 Tablespoons
Yield	8-10 slices	16-20 slices

1. Preheat the oven to 350°F.
2. Combine the sugar, flour, mustard, and cinnamon. Mix.
3. Add the water, and stir until smooth.
4. Place ham slices in the baking dish you will send to the meal recipients.
5. Spoon the glaze over the top.
6. Cover with tin foil and bake for 1 hour.

Additional favorites include Spaghetti Pie (page 40), Mix & Match Soup (page 139), Lasagna (page 102), Burritos (page 104), and BBQ Meatballs (page 82)

Fun & Fancy Potato Sides

If sending BBQ meatballs, ham or some other entrée that needs a side, choose one of these. Delivered meals must be able to retain their heat for 20-45 minutes: hot potato side dishes do this well, pasta and rice don't (which is why there are no pasta or rice side dishes recommended).

Twice-Baked Potatoes

Ingredients	Quantity	X2	X4
Large baking potatoes	4	8	16
Butter	1/4 cup	1/2 cup	1 cup
Milk	2/3 cup	1-1/3 cups	1-2/3 cups
Cheddar cheese, shredded	1/2 cup	3/4 cup	1 cup
Onion, chopped	2 Tablespoons	1/4 cup	1/2 cup
Salt	1 teaspoon	2 teaspoon	1 Tablespoon
Yield	8 potato halves	16 halves	32 halves

1. Preheat oven to 350°F.
2. Fork the potatoes (to insure they don't explode when cooking).
3. Cook the potatoes in microwave (4 potatoes on high for 12 minutes).
4. Cut the baked potatoes in half and scoop out insides being careful to reserve about 1/8" around the outside edge of each potato shell.
5. In a large mixing bowl, stir the potatoes, butter, milk, onion, and salt. Combination will be slightly lumpy.
6. Fold in the cheddar.
7. Scoop mixture into potato shells.
8. Bake for 20-25 minutes.
9. Sprinkle with paprika and serve hot.

Potato Casserole

My friend, Nancy Fisher, is an awesome cook and an amazing mother of five who entertains on a regular basis. During her daughter, Julia's, senior year in high school, Nancy served a high-carb meal to the girls' basketball team, in her home, before every home game. This is one of my favorite recipes from her collection.

	Quantity	X2	X4
Hashbrown potatoes	1 pound	2 pounds	4 pounds
Butter, melted	1/4 cup	1/2 cup	1 cup
Cream of chicken soup	1 can	2 cans	4 cans
Sour cream	1/2 cup	1 cup	2 cups
Cheddar cheese, shredded	1 cup	2 cups	3 cups
Salt	1/2 teaspoon	1 teaspoon	1-1/2 teaspoon
Pepper	1/8 teaspoon	1/4 teaspoon	1/4 teaspoon
Yield	2 cups	4 cups	8 cups

1. Preheat the oven to 350°F.
2. Mix together all the ingredients.
3. Scoop into casserole dishes.
4. Cover with tin foil and bake for 30 minutes.

Hot Vegetables

Similar to the situation above, we found only two hot vegetable recipes that retain their flavor and heat to the extent required for delivered meals. Both are delicious!

Corn Bake

	Quantity	X2
Corn, all liquid drained	3 cups	6 cups
Milk	1/4 cup	1/2 cup
Egg	1	2
Butter, melted	2 Tablespoons	1/4 cup
Sugar	1/4 cup	1/3 cup
Salt	1/4 teaspoon	1/2 teaspoon
Pepper	dash	1/8 teaspoon
Yield	3 cups	6 cups

1. Preheat the oven to 350°F.
2. Mix all ingredients together and scoop into cooking dishes.
3. Cover with tin foil.
4. Bake for 30 minutes.

French Bean Casserole

French cut beans	2 cans or 1 pound frozen
Milk	1/4 cup
Cream of mushroom soup	1 can
French fried onions	1 cup
Yield	4-6 servings

1. Preheat the oven to 350°F.
2. Mix the beans, milk, and soup together.
3. Pour into a greased 9" pie plate, 1-1/2 quart casserole or an 8x8" pan.
4. Cover and bake for 30 minutes.
5. Remove from oven.
6. Sprinkle the onions over all.
7. Cover tightly with tin foil to keep warm until served.

Fruit Salad Recipes

Creamy Fruit Salad

	Quantity	X2	X4
Package gelatin*	3 ounces box	2 boxes	4 boxes
Instant vanilla pudding	5 ounces box	3 ounces box	2–5 ounces box
Boiling water	1 cup	2 cups	4 cups
Fruit, drain juice*	1 cup	2 cups	4 cups
Whipped top, thawed*	2 cups	4 cups	8 cups
Yield	2 cups	4 cups	8 cups

1. Mix together the dry gelatin and pudding mixes. Stir well.
2. Bring the water to a boil and add it quickly to the above dry mixes.
3. Stir with a whisk until completely smooth.
4. Set the bowl in the freezer to cool for 10 minutes, stirring every 2 minutes with a wire whisk. (Set the timer or you'll lose track of this!)
5. After 10 minutes, add the whip top and stir carefully until no streaks remain.
6. Gently fold in the fruit.
7. Chill in the refrigerator until ready to serve.

Gelatin and fruit options:

- strawberry gelatin and strawberries,
- orange gelatin and mandarin oranges,
- peach gelatin and sliced peaches,
- raspberry gelatin and raspberries.
- lime gelatin and mandarin oranges.

---

*Thaw frozen topping, cover-on, in microwave on medium heat for 1 minute.

Frozen Fruit Cups

Make these in advance to grab from your freezer to send along with any main entrée.

Frozen pink lemonade concentrate	6 ounces	12 ounces
Frozen strawberries, thawed	10 ounces	20 ounces
Fruit cocktail, including juice	15 ounces	29 ounces
Sugar	1/4 cup	1/2 cup
Water	1-1/4 cups	2-1/2 cups
Bananas, sliced	2	4
Yield	12	24

1. Combine lemonade, strawberries, fruit cocktail, sugar, and water; stir well.
2. Add sliced bananas. Stir.
3. Use a soup ladle to fill 5 ounces plastic cups three-quarters full.
4. Line the cups onto cookie sheets and freeze for at least three hours. (The cookie sheets allow you to freeze the cups in layers.)
5. To send out with meal, simply send the frozen fruit cups (they will be ready to eat in 25 minutes).
6. For a fancier dinner, thaw the cups for 25 minutes, then "fluff" with fork. Pour a little clear or pink soda pop over the top and serve immediately.

Cherry Fruit Salad

	Quantity	X2
Cherry gelatin, 3 ounce package	2 boxes	4 boxes
Instant vanilla pudding, 3 ounces package	1 box	2 boxes
Boiling water	3 cups	6 cups
Cherry pie filling, 20 ounces can	1 can	2 cans
Yield	4 cups	8 cups

1. Mix together the dry gelatin and pudding.
2. Bring the water to a boil and add it quickly to the above dry mixes.
3. Stir with a whisk until completely smooth.
4. Add the pie filling and stir well.
5. Place in the refrigerator to chill until time to send it out. Do not freeze.

Fruit Pudding Salad

When you need a quick-to-fix fruit side dish, it doesn't get any easier than this!

	Original	X2
Fruit cocktail, reserve juice	2 cans	4 cans
Instant vanilla pudding mix	1 box	2 boxes
Mini marshmallows	1 cup	2 cups
Whipped topping	2 cups	4 cups
Yield	4 cups	8 cups

1. Mix the fruit juice with the pudding mix.
2. Stir until smooth.
3. Fold in the whipped topping.
4. Gently add the fruit and marshmallows.
5. Refrigerate.

Breads & Biscuits

Easy Bread Sticks

Inexpensive refrigerator biscuits offer a speedy and delicious bread stick solution.

Ingredient	Quantity	X2
Refrigerator biscuits	1 can (10 individual biscuits)	
Garlic salt	to sprinkle over top	
Yield	20	

1. Preheat oven to 425°F.
2. Grease a cookie sheet (may use spray pan coating).
3. Cut biscuits in half.
4. With greased hands, roll out the biscuits into breadsticks.
5. Place each breadstick onto the cookie sheet, leaving 2" between.
6. Sprinkle all with garlic salt.
7. Use fingers to roll each breadstick back and forth until coated all over with garlic salt.
8. Bake for 8-10 minutes, until golden brown.
9. Remove and let cool on racks.

Cheese Garlic Biscuits

These taste remarkably like the ones they serve at Red Lobster.

Ingredient	Quantity	X2
Biscuit mix	2 cups	4 cups
Milk	2/3 cup	1-1/3 cups
Cheddar cheese, shredded	3/4 cup	1-1/2 cups
Butter, melted	1/4 cup	1/2 cup
Garlic powder	1/2 teaspoon	3/4 teaspoon
Yield	12 biscuits	24 biscuits

1. Preheat oven to 425°F.
2. Use a fork to mix together the biscuit mix, milk, and cheese.
3. Drop onto greased cookie sheets, at least 1" apart.
4. Bake 8-10 minutes until golden brown.
5. Remove from oven.
6. While they are cooking, melt the butter and mix in the garlic.
7. When the biscuits come out of the oven, brush this mixture on top before removing to cooling racks.

Caution: Best served within 2 hours. These do not freeze well.

Dessert Recipes

Cherry Cheese Cakes

Ingredient	X2	X4	X8
Vanilla wafers	6	12	24
Cream cheese	8 ounces	16 ounces	32 ounces
Sugar	1/4 cup	1/2 cup	1 cup
Vanilla	1/2 teaspoon	1 teaspoon	2 teaspoons
Eggs	1	2	4
Cherry pie filling	1 can	1 can	2 cans
Yield	6 cheesecakes	12 cheesecakes	24 cakes

1. Preheat oven to 350°F.
2. Line each muffin cup with a foil liner.
3. Place a wafer in each liner.
4. Using the electric mixer, beat the cream cheese, vanilla, and sugar until it is smooth.
5. Add the eggs and stir again.
6. Spoon this combination over the wafers, filling each cup 3/4 full.
7. Bake for 20 minutes.
8. Remove from pans and chill in the refrigerator.
9. Top with a dollop of cherry pie filling.

Oatmeal Caramel Bars

Makes one 9x13" pan.

Note: This recipe cannot be doubled; instead, assemble two pans, one at a time and then bake side by side.

Ingredient	Quantity
Flour	2 cups
Oatmeal	2 cups
Brown sugar	1-1/2 cups
Baking soda	1 teaspoon
Salt	1/4 teaspoon
Butter, room temperature	3 sticks (1-1/2 cups)
Chocolate chips	2 cups (12 ounces)
Caramel ice cream topping	1 cup
Yield	9x13" pan

1. Preheat oven to 350°F.
2. Combine the flour, oatmeal, sugar, soda, and salt.
3. Add the butter and mix until mixed but still lumpy.
4. Press 1/2 of the mixture into a 9x13" pan. (You do not need to grease or flour this pan.)
5. Bake this crust for 8-10 minutes.
6. Remove from oven and sprinkle with the chips.
7. Drizzle over the caramel ice cream topping.
8. Sprinkle all the remaining crumbs over the top.
9. Bake for an additional 15-20 minutes. Do not over bake.
10. Let cool at least 30 minutes before cutting.

Cherries in the Snow

Ingredient	Quantity
Graham crackers, crumbled	24
Butter	1/2 cup (1 stick)
Cream cheese	8 ounces
Sugar	1 cup
Vanilla	1 teaspoon
Whipped topping	4 cups
Miniature marshmallows	3 cups
Cherry pie filling	1 can
Yield	45 muffin-cup-size servings

1. Combine the crumbs and butter.
2. Line muffin pans with paper cups.
3. Press the crust combination into the bottom of muffin cups.
4. Using electric mixer, cream together the cheese, sugar, and vanilla.
5. Using just a rubber spatula, fold in the whipped topping and marshmallows.
6. Spread this combination over the crust.
7. Top with the cherries.
8. Refrigerate until ready to serve.

Chapter 8

Soup, Sandwiches, Fruit, Vegetable, Salad & Potato Bars

*The reason restaurant salad bars often disappoint
is because we have a unique set of favorites,
and they can't read our minds.*

This chapter contains a smorgasbord of ideas including the basic recipes and how-to's that will allow you to serve small or large groups using the fruits and vegetables you have on hand. You will discover how to make hundreds of interesting and tasty combinations using my Mix & Match recipes for:

- Soup
- Super salads
- Submarine sandwiches
- Fruit filling
- Fruit pops
- Potato bar

Serving family portions is pretty straightforward, but if you are hosting a food bar for a crowd, take advantage of the strategies in this chapter along with the quantity chart on page 146 and the decorating tips in chapter 9.

Buying Fruits & Vegetables

Fresh produce tastes great, adds variety to our menus, and provides vitamins, minerals, and the fiber our bodies need. In our rush to get dinner on the table we sometimes forget the importance of serving these dietary components with every meal.

Growing your own garden is a terrific option for those who have the space and time to do it. For the rest of us, we can still enjoy fresh fruits and vegetables by shopping farmer's markets, roadside stands, and taking advantage of seasonal fruit in the local produce department. Start watching for seasonal values in your area and make notes in your Kitchen Notebook so you know which week they're likely to come around again next year.

During produce slumps, choose a variety of sale-priced fruits and vegetables and then fill in with a selection from the canned and frozen food departments.

While I usually dress up fruit for guests, if you were to stop by our house at mealtime on most days, on the table you would probably find a fruit platter (described later in the chapter) or fresh fruit being served in small glass dessert dishes set to the upper left of each place setting without added sauces. Fruit is simply delicious.

Likewise, vegetables are usually presented either raw or cooked until tender-crisp and then served without sauces. On rare occasions we indulge and serve vegetables with melted butter or a cream sauce (list on page 133).

Vegetables

Earlier in this book I shared vegetable recipes for side dishes like corn bake and green bean casserole, raw veggie accents like Ranch, salsa and dill dip. In a moment we'll address salads, but here I want to mention the most common vegetable sauces and where to find them in the book:

- Béchamel (page 63) is a vegetable sauce that also works great with most meats and pastas.
- Béarnaise sauce (page 169) accents pastas, meats, and vegetables as equals.
- Cheese sauce (page 62) tastes great on everything from potatoes to greens to pasta.
- Hollandaise (page 184) is ideal for egg dishes, but is also awesome over vegetables and meat.
- Maltaise (page 187) is best over broccoli, but can also be combined with other head vegetables.
- Mornay (page 63) accents eggs, crepes, lobster, spinach, and many other vegetables.

A long list of additional vegetable sauce ideas may be found at http://en.wikipedia.org/wiki/Sauce. I've included my favorite recipes for the most common sauces in the main body or substitutions guide of this book, but anytime your recipe calls for a different one, just do a Google search and you'll find many recipes from which to choose.

Super Salads Every Time

Homemade salads far surpass restaurant salad bars because your preferences rule the roost. Who cares what other people want? Your salad fixings will feature your own favorites. Of course, when hosting guests, be sure to include your favs, the basics you would find at any restaurant salad bar.

My sister, Marcia, shared the best salad recipe I've ever come across. Simply toss together equal parts of every salad ingredient, including as many unique tastes as you like, then drizzle with your favorite dressing. The equal amounts of all flavors, including greens, yields a remarkably robust taste.

Salad Dressings

One fun advantage of owning our espresso café is creating "house" dressings. But you, too, can play around with dressings until finding your own perfect blend. Make your traditional favorites from scratch, with the recipes that follow, or mix existing dressings to create your own unique flavors. My favorite combination is equal parts of Ranch and Blue Cheese dressings. I'm not a big fan of Blue Cheese by itself, but in this mix, it rocks.

Fast French Dressing

Ingredients	Quantity	X____
Olive oil	1 cup	
Red or white wine vinegar	3/4 cup	
Dijon	1 Tablespoon	
Onion powder	1 teaspoon	
Thyme	1 teaspoon	
Salt & Pepper	To Taste	
Yield	1 cup	

Whir in blender at low speed until mixed but not expanded.

Ranch Dressing Mix

This is a terrific mix to have on hand for homemade salad dressings and hors d'oeuvres. The homemade version costs a fraction of its bottled equivalent.

Ingredients	Quantity	X____
Nonfat dry milk powder	1/4 cup	
Garlic powder	1 teaspoon	
Onion powder	1 teaspoon	
Sugar	1 teaspoon	
Dill weed	1/2 teaspoon	
Salt	1/2 teaspoon	
Dry mustard	1/8 teaspoon	
Yield	1/3 cup	

Mix all ingredients and store indefinitely in a moisture proof, air-tight container at room temperature.

Use Instructions:	Quantity for regular version	Quantity for nonfat version
Dry mix	1/3 cup	2 Tablespoons
Mayonnaise	1 cup	—
Fat-free mayonnaise	—	1/3 cup
Water	1/4 cup	—
Lemon juice	4 teaspoons	—
Liquid nonfat milk	—	1 cup
Yield	1 cup	1 cup

Combine all ingredients and mix well. Refrigerate for a minimum of 3 hours to blend flavors.

Creamy Italian Dressing Mix

Ingredients	Quantity	X4
Nonfat dry milk powder	2 Tablespoons	1/2 cup
Italian seasoning	1 teaspoon	1 Tablespoon
Garlic powder	1/2 teaspoon	2 teaspoons
Onion powder	1/2 teaspoon	2 teaspoons
Yield	2 Tablespoons	1/2 cup

Combine all ingredients and store indefinitely in a moisture-proof, airtight container at room temperature.

Use Instructions:	Quantity for regular version	Quantity for fat-free version
Dry mix	2 Tablespoons	2 Tablespoons
Mayonnaise	1 cup	
Fat-free mayonnaise		1/2 cup
Water	6 Tablespoons	1/2 cup
Yield	1-1/4 cups	1-1/3 cups

Blend all ingredients well and refrigerate for several hours before serving. Keep refrigerated.

Thousand Island/Russian Dressing

Ingredients	Quantity	X____
Mayonnaise	1 cups	
Ketchup	3 Tablespoons	
Sweet pickle relish	3 Tablespoons	
Mustard powder	1/2 teaspoon	
Onion powder	1/2 teaspoon	
Red pepper sauce	Dash	
Yield	1 cup	

Whir in blender at low speed until mixed but not expanded.

The Potato Bar

Creating a people-pleasing potato bar is not at all difficult and it makes for a fun meal.

Oven: Scrub, salt, poke with a fork, then wrap each potato in tin foil. Place in a 375°F oven, directly on the racks, for 70-120 minutes. The bigger and more potatoes you are baking, the longer it takes. **Note:** Potatoes can be held hot for up to 2 hours, but are practically inedible if under baked. Allow extra time. Serve the potatoes in the foil, allowing each guest to unwrap her own.

Microwave: If you are serving only a few potatoes, microwave them. Scrub, salt, and poke with a fork, but don't wrap in tin foil. Allow 5-6 minutes each or 15-18 minutes on high for four medium potatoes. Poke with a fork to test for doneness.

Toppings: For toppings, set out a smorgasbord including a wide variety of the following and any others you desire, or ask guests to bring all the toppings while you focus on the potatoes, beverages, and dessert.

- sour cream, butter, salt, and pepper
- shredded cheeses
- bacon bits
- chives
- chopped onions
- chili
- mushrooms, sautéed
- olives
- avocado slices or chunks
- broccoli or cauliflower florets
- sweet bell pepper
- jalapenos
- chipotle
- Ranch dressing (recipe on page 135)
- garlic butter (page 98)
- queso dip (page 196)
- shredded ham
- grilled or creamed chicken
- shredded or crumbled ground beef
- stroganoff or beef tips
- blue cheese
- chopped fresh herbs
- pesto
- sautéed spinach with garlic
- salsa
- sun dried tomatoes
- mixed grilled vegetables
- sliced toasted almonds
- chopped water chestnuts

If you have leftover potatoes, you'll love the following soup recipe, which provides lots of fun options for using them up.

Mix & Match Soup

Soup may have been the original comfort food, and it's still a favorite, especially on cold winter days. The following recipe allows you to use whatever you have on hand to make a delicious soup in minutes. And, as you can see, it is easy to create multiple, unique soups, from just this one recipe. To impress guests, buy personal-size bread bowls from your local bakery. Freeze until it's time to thaw, fill with hot soup, and serve for that special meal.

Ingredients	Quantity	X____
Raw Meat: Ham, chicken breast, venison, round steak	1 cup diced	
Starch: Raw potato cubes, uncooked spiral pasta slightly undercooked rice	3 cups	
Soup Veggies: Celery, onions carrots	1 cup diced total	
Liquid I: Bouillon, stock, canned soup, left-over gravy, etc.	2 cups	
Liquid II: Juice, wine, or more of Liquid I	1 cup	
Seasonings (choose 2-3*)	1 teaspoon each	
Butter	4 Tablespoons	
Flour	4 Tablespoons	
Milk	2 cups	
Salt & pepper	To taste	
Yield	6 cups	

Use Instructions:

Combine the meat, starch, veggies, and liquid in a large kettle. Bring to boil. Cook over medium heat 15 minutes. Stir in the soup base, and seasonings. In a separate pan, melt butter over medium-low heat. Whisk in flour with a fork, and cook, stirring constantly until thick, about 1 minute. Slowly stir in milk so as not to allow lumps to form. Continue stirring over medium-low heat until thick, 4 to 5 minutes. Stir the milk mixture into the stockpot, and cook soup until heated through. Serve immediately or freeze for future use.

Your Own Sandwich & Sub Shop at Home

My friend, Lynn Hartzell, often inspires me. One day while visiting her home at lunchtime, she casually walked over to her refrigerator, opened the door, and pulled out, basically, a professional sandwich shop.

I returned home from that trip and promptly put her idea to work. I added a simple plastic storage container, just larger than a shoe box, to my own refrigerator. Inside that box I loaded our favorite meats, cheeses, condiments, and veggies—everything required to make my family's favorite sandwiches.

After purchasing our restaurant in 2002, I took it to a new level. To this day we still use the sub-shop-in-a-box approach for making customer subs. We store the loaves at room temperature and the rest in plastic boxes in the refrigerator below the work station, ready to grab, all at once, in a flash.

Create your own box, letting your family's favorite ingredients be your guide. The beauty of a sub shop at home is that you can serve a side of fresh fruit (instead of chips), something few sandwich shops can offer.

Fruit

The following recipes enable you to dress-up or use-up any fruit you have on hand. Before I get to them, however, I want to share one of my favorite, money-saving shortcuts that isn't a recipe. It's my fruit platter. I literally create my own fruit platters at home for less than 25% of the cost of deli platters. Here's how:

1. Buy an empty display tray from the deli or a restaurant supply store.
2. Stock up on your favorite melons, berries, grapes, and a fresh pineapple.
3. Spend 30 minutes chopping them all up.
4. Create one beautiful fruit platter (using about 1/4 of the fruit).
5. Store the remainder in zip top bags in the fruit drawer.

While I let the kids munch on whole fruits, like apples, oranges and so on, I reserve the fruit displays for meals and appetizers.

Fruit Toppings and Dip Ideas   When you decide to splurge, and top your fruit with calories, here are some fast and fancy options.

Honey Syrup

Simply heat some honey in the microwave for a few seconds and pour a few tablespoons over the fruit you have on hand; stir to coat and serve.

Tangy Fruit Topping

1 cup regular or low fat mayonnaise

1 cup regular or fat free whipped topping

Whisk together and serve over any fruit combination.

Apple Dip

7 ounces jar marshmallow cream

8 ounces regular or Neufchâtel cream cheese

1 teaspoon vanilla

Blend until smooth and serve as a dip.

Whipped Dressing

1 cup whipped topping

1 teaspoon sugar

1/2 teaspoon mustard

1/2 teaspoon vanilla

Mix & Match Frozen Fruit Pops

These are especially popular with kids, and their parents.

Ingredients	Quantity	X____
Frozen juice concentrate	1/2 cup	
Milk	2/3 cup	
Banana	1	
Yield	8 popsicles	

Combine ingredients in blender container and whir on high until smooth. Pour into 8 popsicle molds and freeze until firm (about 3 hours). When using orange juice concentrate, the addition of one tablespoon sugar to the blender creates an Orange Dreamsicle. The banana is always optional.

Mix & Match Fruit Filling

Fresh, frozen or canned fruit work well in this quick-to-fix fruit sauce. Use your favorite combination as a pie filling, atop a crushed graham cracker crust in a 9x9" pan, or over ice cream.

Ingredients	Quantity	X____
White sugar	1 cup	
Cornstarch	2 Tablespoons	
Water	1 cup	
Vanilla	1 teaspoon	
Fruit*	3 cups	
Yield	2 cups, enough for one pie	

*Fruit options include apple slices, seedless berries, and other fruits usually found in dessert pies.

Boil the sugar, cornstarch, and water, stirring until thick. Add the vanilla and fruit. Stir well. Serve over shortcake or ice cream or spoon into a prepared pie crust and chill. Top with whipped topping.

Seasonal Guide to Fruit

Produce Item	Best Month(s) to Buy					
Fruit:	**Jan/ Feb**	**Mar/ April**	**May/ June**	**July/ Aug**	**Sept/ Oct**	**Nov/ Dec**
Apples	x	x			x	
Avocados	x	x	x		x	x
Bananas	x	x	x	x	x	x
Blueberries			x	x		
Cherries			x	x		
Grapes				x	x	x
Grapefruit	x	x	x			x
Lemons			x	x	x	
Limes			x	x	x	
Melons	x	x	x			
Oranges	x	x	x	x	x	
Peaches			x	x	x	
Pears				x	x	x
Pineapple	x	x	x			
Plums			x	x	x	
Raspberries	x	x	x			
Strawberries	x	x	x			

Seasonal Guide to Vegetables

Produce Item	Best Month(s) to Buy					
Vegetables:	Jan/ Feb	Mar/ April	May/ June	July/ Aug	Sept/ Oct	Nov/ Dec
Beans			x	x		
Broccoli	x				x	x
Brussels sprouts	x				x	x
Carrots	x	x	x	x	x	x
Corn				x	x	x
Cucumber			x	x		
Eggplant				x	x	
Lettuce	x	x	x	x	x	x
Peas	x	x	x	x		
Peppers				x	x	x
Potatoes	x	x	x	x	x	x
Spinach	x	x				
Summer squash			x	x	x	
Sweet potatoes					x	x
Tomato			x	x		
Winter squash					x	x

If you are just getting started in the entertaining business, trying to figure out how much food to make can be a challenge. The following guidelines will help you avoid wasting money. The weights and measurements listed refer to food in its uncooked state. If you are given a range of servings, assume that women and children consume the smaller servings and teenagers and men the larger. Happy hosting!

Hostess Quantity Chart	
Soup as side dish	3/4 cup per person
Soup as main dish	1-1/2 cups per person
Fish	4 to 6 ounces per person
Poultry on bone	I pound per person
Boneless poultry	6 to 8 ounces per person
Beef on bone	6 to 8 ounces per person
Boneless beef	4 to 6 ounces per person
Rice	2 ounces per person
Pasta as side dish	1 ounce per person
Pasta as main dish	2 ounces per person
Vegetables	1/2 to 3/4 cup per person
Lettuce	Large head per 6 people
Dinner rolls	2 per person
Bread as side dish	1 loaf per 10 people
Main dish sauce	2 tablespoons per person
Dessert sauce	2 tablespoons per person
Fruit salad	1/2 cup per person
Ice cream	3/4 to 1 cup per person
Dessert pie	Serves 6 to 8
Two-layer cake	Serves 10 to 12
9 by 13-inch cake	Serves 12 to 16
Cheesecake	Serves 8 to 12
Coffee	2 to 3 cups per coffee drinker

Chapter 9

Desserts, Drizzles &
Table Top Displays

*It never ceases to amaze me
what a little drizzle can do for a latte,
or what an elevated platter can do for a cake.*

I have always loved to put on a good show, and serving beautiful food on a breathtaking table is my idea of great fun! The following are some of the ways you can dress up just about anything.

Be Ready

If you do nothing else with this chapter, do this:

1. Identify one punch recipe you love.
2. Identify one appetizer you can make fast and feel great about serving.
3. Add the ingredients of both to your Master Shopping List.
4. Always keep the needed supplies on hand.

What are your favorites? Mine are Sherbet Punch and Shrimp Dip Platter. I am never without the ingredients to whip these up for impromptu hosting situations. Obviously, I could make anything in my recipe repertoire, but having a clear idea of my "standard fallbacks" allows me to confidently say, "Sure! Why don't you just stop over in a few minutes?"

Sherbet Punch

Pick a color: pink for strawberry/raspberry, orange for orange, and green for lime. Pour 2 liters of the matching-color Schweppes Ginger Ale into a punch bowl or party glasses. Top with scoops of matching sherbet to equal one pint per 2 liters of Ale. Serve frothy.

Shrimp Dip Platter

Spread 8 ounces of cream cheese onto the center of a large, glass serving platter, leaving a 1" edge. Fan Ritz crackers around the outside edge. Layer shrimp cocktail sauce over the cream cheese, leaving 1/2" edge. Quick thaw 4 ounces of tailless, cooked salad shrimp, pat dry, and evenly distribute over sauce. Sprinkle with 1/4 cup shredded cheddar. Serve.

Shrimp Cocktail Sauce

Mix together 1/2 cup ketchup, 3 tablespoons pickle relish, 1 teaspoon mustard, and a dash each of Worcestershire sauce, Tabasco sauce, and sugar.

Napkins

I use one basic napkin move for practically every occasion. I sometimes go fancy, but mostly, I poke my finger into the center of a cloth napkin, fluff the fabric a bit, and drop the center point into the bottom of a water or wine glass. It looks awesome and is super fast.

To find fancier folds, search "napkin folds" on the Internet. You can do some really fun stuff by following simple diagrams.

Impressive Table Displays

There are entire books written on this topic, but here is the quick version of my favorite tip:

1. Purchase two matching tablecloths for your largest table size.
2. Use one as the base, with cloth draping over the sides, like usual.
3. Find boxes of varying sizes to create pedestals on the table.
4. Cover the ugly boxes with your second tablecloth, using the excess to created billows, and tucking the raw edges under.
5. Before adding the food, add a few themed decorations—flower petals, candles or something like the International ideas included in chapter 6.

I know this is super easy, but it's way impressive! If you don't believe me, search Google images for beautiful table settings: except for caterers or classy restaurants, most are flat and boring with a lot of pretty food. By adopting this one simple change to your entertaining repertoire, you move into an elite class of hostesses.

Drizzles

Anything looks better with a drizzle! In our espresso café, we use a consistent up, down, up, down pattern (like a fancy "M"), but other designs include circles, stripes, and squiggles.

Drizzles work magic and just three flavor bottles satisfy most dessert needs: chocolate, caramel or strawberry. Use homemade (pages 155-156) or store-bought ice cream syrups.

Drizzles work best if added one serving at a time and aren't just for desserts. Next time you serve a fresh tossed salad, do it in single serving bowls adding a pattern of colorful salad dressings drizzled over the top. Also, top individual bowls of soup with an artful garnish of unsweetened whipping cream and a sprig of parsley or any other herb that compliments the flavor.

Ice Cream Cakes

I already shared my recipe for Mexican Fried Ice Cream Cake on page 103 and the following recipe produces one that can be made to suit the guest of honor and costs less than half of its purchased alternative.

Frozen Mud Pie

Ingredients	Quantity	X4
Chocolate cream-filled cookies or graham crackers	16	32
Instant coffee granules, optional	1 teaspoon	2 teaspoons
Butter	3 Tablespoons	5 Tablespoons
Ice cream	2+ flavors	2+ flavors
Walnuts or pecans	1 cup	2 cups
Ice cream toppings such as chocolate and caramel	1 cup	2 cups
Whipped topping	8 ounces	8 ounces
Yield	6 to 8 servings	10 to 16 servings

Crush cookies and coffee granules; combine with butter and press into an ungreased 9" round or 9x13" pan. Bake in 350°F oven for 8 minutes. Remove and let cool. Press one layer of your favorite ice cream, about 1/2" thick, onto crust. Top with a generous sprinkling of nuts, then a steady, thin drizzle of both toppings. Layer on a different kind of ice cream, then repeat the nuts and toppings. Continue layers until ice cream is within 1 inch of pan rim. Finish with a generous layer of whipped topping, sprinkling on nuts, and making a final decorative drizzle pattern with the toppings. Freeze and then cover with freezer-quality plastic wrap.

Dessert Pizzas

I love the fun and decorating opportunities provided by dessert pizzas. I often use the fresh fruit pizza itself as a centerpiece—taking time to arrange the fruit pieces in a pattern moving from a small target in the center to an entire edge-full of the same fruit-type around the rim. These are absolutely delicious to look at, as well as to eat. Here are a few of my personal favorites.

Apple Pizza

Make peanut butter cookie dough from your favorite recipe, but instead of making individual cookies, spread it on a greased pizza pan and bake at 325°F until just cooked. Frost this with a combination of 8 ounces cream cheese mixed together until smooth with 1/2 cup brown sugar and 1 teaspoon cinnamon. Top this with one can of apple pie filling. Drizzle with caramel ice cream topping.

Fruit Pizza

Make sugar cookie dough from your favorite recipe, but instead of making individual cookies, spread it on a greased pizza pan and bake at 325°F until just cooked. Frost this with a combination of 8 ounces cream cheese mixed together until smooth with 1/2 cup powdered sugar and 1 teaspoon vanilla. Top this with hardy fruit pieces* in any pattern that suits you. Drizzle with honey.

*Hardy fruits include sliced berries, halved grapes, cubed melons, and pineapple, and from-the-can, drained, mandarin oranges. Do not use bananas, apples or other quickly-discoloring fruit.

Black Forest Pizza

Make a brownie mix from your favorite recipe, but instead of using a square pan, spread half of the batter onto a greased pizza pan and bake at 325°F until just cooked. Frost this with a combination of 8 ounces cream cheese mixed together until smooth with 1/2 cup powdered sugar and 1 teaspoon vanilla. Top this with a can of cherry pie filling. Drizzle with chocolate syrup.

Chocolate Chip Dream Pizza

Make chocolate chip cookie dough from you favorite recipe, but instead of making individual cookies, spread it on a greased pizza pan and bake at 325°F until just cooked. Immediately prior to serving, add a scoop of ice cream to each piece and drizzle with chocolate syrup.

Fast Frostings

Mix & Match Frosting Mix

Your special baked goods will shine with these easy, inexpensive, and delightful frostings. They can be made for roughly a quarter of the price of canned frosting and they taste better and have fewer preservatives, too.

Ingredients	Quantity for white frosting	Quantity for chocolate frosting
Powdered sugar	3 cups	3 cups
Shortening	1/2 cup	1/2 cup
Cocoa	—	3/4 cup
Hot tap water	4 teaspoons	3 Tablespoons
Extract of choice	1 teaspoon	1 teaspoon
Yield	1-1/2 cups	1-1/2 cups

If making chocolate frosting, stir together the sugar and cocoa until well blended, then proceed as follows. Cream the sugar and shortening, adding water as needed until of spreadable consistency. Add the extract as follows:

Vanilla: 1 teaspoon

Peppermint: 1 teaspoon, a few drops of green food coloring

Almond: 1 teaspoon. Sprinkle finished dessert with slivered or sliced almonds

Maple: 1 teaspoon

Other Frosting Flavors:

Mocha: Add 1/2 Tablespoon fine instant coffee granules to chocolate frosting; mix well.

Lemon: Replace the water with lemon juice, and omit the extract.

Orange: Add 2 egg yolks and 1 teaspoon grated orange peel, and reduce the water to 2 Tablespoons.

Peanut butter: Replace the shortening in the white frosting recipe with peanut butter and increase the water to 1/2 cup.

Syrups from Scratch

I cannot even tell you how stress-busting it is to know that you can make dessert syrups from scratch anytime.

We have often impressed our guests with basic ice cream, scooped into parfait or dessert cups, surrounded by a selection of hot, fresh, homemade syrups. The following are a few of our favorites, but don't forget the Crème de Menthe syrup on page 50. Also, if you have any interesting sandwich jam on hand, heat it a bit, being sure not to boil it, and then stir it well and serve it as another syrup option. If you also put out a few sliced bananas, strawberries, and some pineapple cubes, you've got yourself banana splits par excellence.

Chocolate Syrup

This truly excellent syrup can be made for less than a fourth the cost of the commercial brands.

Ingredients	Quantity	Quantity for fat-free version
Liquid nonfat milk		1 cup
Milk	1 cup	
Butter	1 Tablespoon	
White sugar	2 cups	2 cups
Unsweetened cocoa powder	1/2 cup	1/2 cup
Vanilla	1/2 teaspoon	1/2 teaspoon
Yield	2 cups, for a total of 1,940 calories/ 22 grams fat	2 cups, for a total of 1,790 calories/ 4 grams fat

Combine all ingredients in a blender and whir for a few seconds until cocoa powder is blended. Heat through, on stove top or in microwave, stirring often, until hot. Do not boil. Serve hot or cold over ice cream, or add a tablespoon to a glass of cold or hot milk for chocolate milk or hot cocoa.

Caramel Syrup

This excellent sauce goes together quickly in the microwave.

Ingredients	Quantity	Quantity for fat-free version
Butter, melted	4 Tablespoons	
Corn syrup	2 Tablespoons	1/3 cup
Brown sugar	1 cup	1/2 cup
Milk or cream	1/3 cup	
Liquid nonfat milk		1/4 cup
Cornstarch		1 teaspoon
Vanilla	1 teaspoon	1 teaspoon
Yield	1-1/2 cups	2/3 cup

Instructions for Original Version

Blend together butter, corn syrup, brown sugar, and milk, and microwave on high for 3 to 4 minutes, stirring after each 60-second interval. Add vanilla and stir to blend. Serve warm or cold.

Instructions for Fat-Free Version

Mix the corn syrup, brown sugar, and 3 tablespoons of the liquid nonfat milk and microwave on high until it boils. Stir and microwave on high for 1 minute longer. Combine the remaining tablespoon of nonfat milk with 1 teaspoon cornstarch and stir to blend. Stirring the heated mixture constantly, gradually add the cornstarch combination. Microwave on high for 30 seconds longer; stir. Add vanilla and serve warm or cold.

Chapter 10

Breakfast & Brunch

How you start your morning tends to influence
the rest of your day. Start it in style!

Again in this chapter you will find some of my favorite "Mix & Match" recipes, this time for:

- Quiche
- Muffins
- Fruit smoothies
- Pancakes
- Crepes

Prior to the birth of our third child, Timothy, I made up several batches of muffins. After his homecoming, I would take out some muffins the night before, placing them in the center of the table on a covered platter, and head to bed. In the morning, even if I couldn't make it to the kitchen in time, Dave and the older two children would have something homemade to eat.

The recipes in this chapter work for exhausted mornings during the postpartum period, but they are also great for party brunches and special mornings shared with overnight guests.

Mix & Match Crustless Quiche

If I could only give you one breakfast recipe, it would be this excellent, easy quiche, because it has saved me countless times! Often, when entertaining overnight guests, we stay up into the wee hours visiting, and then squeeze every minute of sleep out of the morning before launching into the next full day. Crustless Quiche takes less than 3 minutes to assemble then cooks for 60 minutes, giving guests time to shower and dress, and the cook time to bake muffins and make smoothies before it comes out of the oven, looking picture perfect.

Ingredients	Quantity	X____
Eggs	3	
Milk	1-1/3 cups	
Butter, melted	1/4 cup	
Biscuit mix	1/2 cup	
Pepper	Sprinkle	
Yield	4-6 servings	

Whir the eggs through pepper on high 45 seconds. Pour into greased 8" or 9" pie plate. Bake at 350°F for 60 minutes.

Optional Add-Ins

Prior to pouring the egg mixture into a 9" pie plate, layer in any or all of the following options.

- 1 cup of cooked, diced meats like sausage, ham, crumbled bacon or comparable
- 1 cup of shredded cheese like cheddar, American, and Mozzarella
- 1/2 cup of sautéed vegetables like onions, green peppers or similar

Mix & Match Muffins

While the quiche is baking throw together a batch of your your special muffin recipe, or whip up a new family favorite by choosing your children's favorite ingredients and following these measurements and instructions.

Note: The #1 reason muffins fail is due to overbeating. Mix gently, with a wooden spoon, by hand, only until ingredients are combined. Never use an electric mixer for muffins.

Choose your grain:
- 2 cups flour or
- 1 cup flour, 1 cup oatmeal or
- 1 cup flour, 1 cup flake cereal

Add and whisk together:
- 1 teaspoon baking powder and
- 1 teaspoon baking soda and
- 1/4 teaspoon salt and either
- 1 teaspoon of cinnamon or
- 1 teaspoon of pumpkin pie spice or
- 2 teaspoons grated orange or lemon rind

Choose and add your sweetener:
- 1/2 cup sugar or
- 3/4 cup brown sugar or
- 2/3 cup honey (reduce liquid to 3/4 cup)
- 2/3 cup molasses (reduce liquid to 3/4 cup)

Choose and add your liquid:
- 1 cup milk, buttermilk or
- 1 cup fruit juice or
- 1/2 and 1/2 milk and juice or
- 1/2 and 1/2 milk and sour cream

Choose and add your eggs:
- 2 eggs or
- Egg substitute

Choose and add your oil:
- 1 cup liquid oil or
- 1 cup butter, room temperature or
- 1 cup applesauce or
- 1 cup pumpkin pie filling

Choose and add 1 cup (or 1/2 and 1/2) extras:
- chopped nuts
- dates, raisins or Craisins®
- berries
- coconut
- fried and crumbled bacon bits
- finely shredded zucchini
- mashed bananas
- chocolate or butterscotch chips

Fold together until just barely blended. Bake in pre-sprayed muffin cups at 350°F for 20-25 minutes or until a toothpick inserted into the center comes out clean.

Fruit Smoothies

While the quiche and muffins finish baking, blend up some frothy fruit smoothies using whatever ingredients you have on hand.

Ingredients	Quantities	X____
Frozen fruit juice concentrate (orange, apple, etc.) or fresh or frozen, thawed fruit (berries, bananas, etc.)	6 ounce can juice or 2 cups fruit	
Milk	1 cup	
Water (eliminate when using fresh or frozen fruit)	1 cup	
Sugar	1/2 cup	
Vanilla	1 teaspoon	
Ice cubes	8	
Yield	4 servings	

Combine desired ingredients in blender container and whir on high until slushy. Serve immediately.

Biscuit Mix for Pancakes, Crepes & Waffles

Use the original version any time a recipe calls for Bisquick®, pancake mix, or muffin mix. The defatted version tastes much like the boxed variety at an incredible savings of 70 grams of fat per recipe. The whole wheat recipe can be substituted cup for cup in recipes calling for biscuit mix.

Ingredients	Quantity for original version	6X	Quantity for defatted version
All-purpose flour	1-7/8 cups	11 cups	1-7/8 cups
Whole wheat flour	—	—	—
Baking powder	4 teaspoons	1/2 cup	4 teaspoons
Salt	1/2 teaspoon	1 Tablespoon	1/2 teaspoon
Shortening	1/3 cup	2 cups	—
Sugar	—	—	2 Tablespoons
Nonfat dry milk powder	—	—	3 Tablespoons
Yield (biscuit mix)	2 cups	12 cups	2 cups

2 cups data: Original @ 1,378 calories/72 grams fat; defatted @ 820 calories/2 grams fat; whole wheat @ 1,606 calories/58 grams fat

Instructions for Original Mixes

Combine dry ingredients, cut in shortening. Store for up to 6 months in an airtight, moisture-proof container at room temperature.

Instructions for Defatted Mix

Combine ingredients and store in an airtight, moisture-proof container at room temperature until needed. Mix requires the addition of 1/3 cup liquid nonfat milk per 2 cups dry biscuit mix. Since liquid nonfat milk cannot be stored at room temperature, add it immediately prior to use and keep any unused batter refrigerated. Make a note on your recipe or on the container of dry mix whenever you use this mix, that 1/3 cup liquid nonfat milk should be added to the recipe. Further defat your life by replacing milk and eggs with liquid nonfat milk and egg substitutes in any recipe.

Recipe options:

Pancakes

Stir together 2 cups mix, 1 cup milk, and 2 eggs until just blended. Cook on hot, ungreased griddle until golden, flipping once.

Crepes

Whip together 2 cups mix, 2 cups milk, and 4 eggs until smooth and lump-free. Cook on hot, greased crepe pan until golden, flipping once.

Waffles

Stir together 2 cups mix, 1-1/2 cups milk, 1/2 cup oil, and 2 eggs (slightly beaten). Bake in a hot, sprayed waffle iron until golden.

Dropped Biscuits

Stir together 2 cups mix and 1 cup milk until just moistened. Bake at 400°F on a greased cookie sheet for 8 to 10 minutes.

Rolled Biscuits

Stir together 2-1/2 cups mix and 2/3 cup milk. Knead ten times, then roll out to 1/2 inches thickness and cut as desired. Bake on a greased cookie sheet at 450°F for 8 to 10 minutes.

Maple Syrup

Create your own maple syrup on the stove top while you make the pancakes and both will be ready at the same time. At one-fourth the price of the leading brand, this syrup can't be beat!

Ingredients	Quantity	X____
Brown sugar	2 cups	
Sugar	1 cup	
Water	1-1/3 cups	
Maple extract	2 teaspoons	
Yield	2-2/3 cups	

Combine the sugars and water in a saucepan over medium-high heat; bring to a boil. Remove from heat and add extract. Pour into a clean jar and refrigerate indefinitely.

Note: This syrup tastes great immediately, but it will get substantially thicker after being in the refrigerator for a few hours.

Appendix I

The Substitutions & Equivalents Guide

*The money- and time-saving opportunities
in this section alone will save you the cost
of the book many times over.*

Have you ever realized mid-recipe that you were out of evaporated milk, cornstarch or some other important ingredient? Or have you noticed that many of the recipes in today's cookbooks, magazines, and newspapers call for one or more unusual, expensive, or hard-to-find items? What do you do? A trip to the store is time consuming and more often results in you buying more items than you originally intended. Purchasing just one "gourmet" ingredient for that fabulous-sounding recipe you just found can cost as much as an entire bag of groceries, and surrendering to take-out food—yet again—is a big drain on the budget.

There's no reason to give up on dinner plans or the fun of trying new recipes just because you lack a certain ingredient. By knowing which ingredients can be substituted for which, you can achieve kitchen freedom—and realize tremendous savings. You can also gain more control over the fat content of your diet by learning which low-fat foods can replace the high-fat items.

In the pages that follow, you'll find an A to Z guide featuring more than five hundred ingredients and foods from baking powder and baby food to shortening and soy sauce. If you don't have a particular item, look it up alphabetically by name and see what you can use as a substitute. If the recipe calls for fresh and all you have is dried or frozen, turn to the entry and you can proceed with confidence. If your recipe calls for a pound of apples and all you have are three apples, will you have enough? The answer is, yes! Quantity data is included for most items and can help you shop wisely.

While many of the substitutions on the following pages provide equivalent or superior results, some offer suitable second choices and others change the taste of your final product noticeably. All save a trip to the store in a pinch, most save money, and some save fat grams. The notations below will aid you in deciding which substitutions are feasible for your endeavors.

> **= Equal:** Your recipe will turn out the same or better than if you had used the original ingredient.
>
> **@ Like:** The final product may vary slightly in either taste or texture. This difference may often go completely unnoticed.
>
> **! Emergency:** These work but will change the final product noticeably. Please do not assume that it will "ruin" the recipe: it will just be "different" from the recipe you are used to. I often actually prefer these "change-of pace" outcomes.
>
> **> Less Fat:** While these change the taste of your recipes slightly, they are honestly "good" substitutions and worth trying. There are some very fun tastes available with less fat using these options.

The ones that do not save money are included to save you fat grams or time in cases where you would have to make a trip to the store if a replacement could not be identified.

"Sugar" refers to white, granulated; "rice" refers to white, long-grain; and "flour" refers to unbleached all-purpose flour, unless otherwise noted.

Accent

1 ounce = 5 Tablespoons

Allspice

1 ounce = 4 Tablespoons
@ equal parts of cinnamon, clove, nutmeg

Amaretti Crumbs

1 cup crushed @ 1 cup crushed almond
biscotti, 1/4 teaspoon almond extract

Amaretto

! almond flavoring

Anchovy Paste

1 Tablespoon = 5 puréed anchovy filets

Anise

1 ounce = 5 Tablespoons
! fennel
! tarragon

Apples

1 medium apple = 6 ounces
1 pound fresh = 3 medium apples
1 pound fresh = 3 cups sliced or chopped
4 pounds fresh = 1 pound dried

Apple Juice

! equal parts white grape juice

Apricots

1 cup = 5 to 13 apricots
5-1/2 pounds fresh = 1 pound dried
1 pound fresh = 8 to 12 whole fresh
1 pound dried = 3-1/4 cups
1 pound cooked and drained = 3 cups

Arrowroot

! 1 teaspoon = 1 Tablespoon all purpose flour

Avocado

1 = 1/2 cup mashed

Baby Food

Feeding baby can be simple and inexpensive if you start baby out on the foods your family usually eats. Follow basic guidelines for starting a baby on solids (see any baby care manual or ask your pediatrician). Purée approximately 1/2 cup of the food you are interested in serving and add water, fruit juice, or broth as follows:

- **Fruits:** 1/2 cup cooked, mashed fruit, 3 Tablespoons liquid
- **Vegetables:** 1/2 cup cooked, mashed vegetables, 3 Tablespoons liquid
- **Meat:** 1/2 cup cooked, mashed meat, 5 Tablespoons liquid (meat broth is fine)
- **Starch:** 1/2 cup cooked, mashed rice, potatoes, noodles, etc., 3 Tablespoons liquid

A great advantage to feeding baby a mashed-up version of whatever you're having is that the child becomes acquainted with the foods your family eats instead of with prepared, jarred, expensive baby foods. Also, you are not setting the precedent: "We eat one thing and you eat another," which is a sure way to develop a finicky eater!

Bacon

8 slices = 1/2 cup cooked and crumbled
1 ounce bacon usually = 1 slice raw bacon
@> turkey bacon (usually a little more expensive)

Bacon Bits

1 ounce = 1/2 cup cooked and crumbled

Baking Powder

1 pound = 2-1/2 cups
2-1/2 Tablespoons = 1 ounce
1 Tablespoon @ 3/4 teaspoon baking soda, 1-3/4 teaspoons cream of

tartar
1 Tablespoon @ 2 teaspoons cream of tartar, 1 teaspoon baking soda,
1/2 teaspoon salt, 1/2 teaspoon cornstarch
1 Tablespoon ! when eggs are called for in a recipe and you are out
of baking powder, add the egg yolks, reserving the whites. Whip the
whites until stiff, then fold in at the end of the recipe; bake as directed.
Will create a slightly heavier product.

Baking Soda

2 Tablespoons = 1 ounce

Bananas

1 pound = 2 large = 5 small
1 medium = 1 cup mashed
1 cup mashed = 14 ounces
1 cup dried = 3-1/2 ounces

Basil

1 ounce = 1/2 cup
! parsley
! Italian Seasoning

Bay Leaf

1 whole = 1/4 teaspoon crushed

Beans

1 cup dried beans = 2 cups cooked

Béarnaise Sauce

1 cup = 1 cup mayonnaise, 1 Tablespoon onion flakes, 2 teaspoons dried
tarragon, 1/4 teaspoon pepper. Whip, cover, and let meld at least 1 hour.

Beau Monde Seasoning

1 teaspoon @ 1/2 teaspoon salt, dashes of garlic, onion, and celery salts

Béchamel Sauce

Recipe on page 63
@ 1 can cream of mushroom soup, 1/4 cup light cream
@ 1 can cream of celery soup, 1/4 cup light cream

Beef

1 pound cooked = 3 cups ground
1 cup pieces = 6 ounces cooked

Beer/Ale

! chicken broth with dash Worcestershire
! ginger ale or club soda with dash Worcestershire
! white grape juice with dash Worcestershire

Biscotti Crumbs

! equal parts Rusk
! equal parts zwieback

Bitters

! equal parts Worcestershire

Black Pepper

1 ounce = 3 Tablespoons

Blueberries

1 cup = 5-1/4 ounces

Bok Choy

Ribs ! equal parts celery, Napa or green cabbage
Leaves ! equal parts Swiss chard or spinach

Bouillon

1 ounce = 10 teaspoons
Use requirements: 1 to 2 teaspoons + 1 cup water = 1 cup soup
1-1/2 teaspoons bouillon @ 1 Tablespoon soup base
Note: I always substitute "soup base" when a recipe calls for bouillon.
It costs less and gives a more natural taste. Many of the mixes included
here require chicken, beef, or onion soup base or bouillon. Dry soup
bases are sold in 1-pound glass or plastic containers near the bouillon in
most supermarkets.

Bouquet Garni

@ 1 bay leaf, 1/2 teaspoon parsley flakes,
1/4 teaspoon Thyme, 1 Tablespoon pepper in cheesecloth

Bran

1 cup = 2 ounces

Brazil Nuts

2 pounds in shells = 1 pound shelled
1 pound shelled = 3 cups

Bread

1 pound loaf = 12 to 16 slices
1 slice usually = 1 ounce

Bruschetta

= Toast spread with a combination of garlic and olive oil
Recipe on page 99

Butter

1 stick = 4 ounces = 8 Tablespoons
4 sticks = 1 pound = 2 cups
@ margarine
>@ diet margarine
>! Heart Beat spread (cannot be used for frying)
>! Butter buds (liquid butter replacement)
! Butter Flavored Crisco (see can for instructions)
1 cup ! 4/5 cup clarified bacon drippings
1 cup ! 7/8 cup lard
1 cup ! 7/8 cup oil
1 cup ! 14 Tablespoons shortening, 1/2 teaspoon salt

Butterscotch

12 ounces chips = 2 cups sauce @ equal parts caramel sauce

Cabbage

1 pound = 4 cups shredded = 2 cups cooked

Cajun Seasoning

1/2 cup = 1 Tablespoon cayenne, 1 Tablespoon
oregano, 1 Tablespoon pepper, 1 Tablespoon
thyme, 2 Tablespoons paprika, 3 Tablespoons salt

Cake Mixes

I have tried many recipes for dry cake mix equivalent and have found all to be disappointing in one way or another. When boxed mixes go on sale, I stock up on the flavors we enjoy. If I happen to run out, most recipe books offer numerous "from-scratch" cake recipes that taste marvelous and require only a few minutes' effort.

Capers

! equal parts green olives

Caraway

1 ounce = 1/4 cup
! cumin

Cardamom

1 ounce = 5 Tablespoons
! equal parts ginger & cinnamon

Carob Powder

1 cup = 3 ounces
1 pound = 4 cups
Note: Carob delivers a noticeable taste difference and it's usually more expensive, but it is preferred by some for it "healthful" benefit. Substitute 3 Tablespoon carob powder, 2 Tablespoon water for each ounce of chocolate required. Carob is sweeter than unsweetened cocoa, so if you use it to replace unsweetened cocoa, reduce the sugar in the recipe by one-quarter.

Carrots

1 pound = 3 cups shredded = 2-1/2 cups diced

Catsup

See Ketchup

Cayenne

1 ounce = 4 Tablespoon
1/8 teaspoon @ few drops Tabasco sauce
! equal parts hot red pepper sauce

Celery

2 medium stalks = 1 cup diced

Celery Flakes

1 ounce = 3 Tablespoon

Celery Salt

1 ounce = 3 Tablespoon

Celery Seed

1 ounce = 4 Tablespoon
1 teaspoon ! 1/4 cup chopped celery and 1 teaspoon dill seed

Cereals

1 cup flake type = 1 ounce
1 cup granola type = 3-1/2 ounces

Cheese, Bleu

4 ounces = 1 cup crumbled = Roquefort

Cheese, cheddar

1 pound = 4 cups shredded
4 ounces = 1 cup shredded

Cheese, cottage

1 pound = 2 cups
@>nonfat cottage cheese
@ ricotta
! feta or cream cheese

Cheese, Cream

3 ounces = 6 Tablespoons
1 cup 4 Tablespoon low-fat margarine, 1 cup nonfat cottage cheese, a
few drops of liquid nonfat milk: blend on high until smooth.
!> nonfat cream cheese
1 cup ! 1 cup plain yogurt

Cheese, Mozzarella

1 pound = 4 cups shredded
! Monterey Jack

Cheese, Parmesan

1 cup = 3-1/2 ounces
1 pound = 6 cups shredded
@ Romano cheese

Cheese, Ricotta

1 pound = 2 cups
! cream cheese
! cottage cheese, blended until smooth

Cheese, Romano

1 pound = 4 cups
@ Parmesan cheese

Cheez Whiz®

1 cup @ Cube 8 ounces American or cheddar cheese.
Combine in microwave-safe dish with 2 Tablespoons butter, 1/2 Table-spoon sugar, 1/2 cup milk and 1/2 teaspoon mustard. Microwave on high 1 minute at a time, stirring vigorously between, until melted and smooth. Store in refrigerator up to 3 months.

Cherries

I quart fresh = 2 cups pitted
1 pound fresh = about 120 cherries

Cherries, Candied

1 cup = 7 ounces

Chicken Meat

Loosely packed . . .
10 ounce breast = 1 cup cooked, de-boned, and diced meat 3 pounds whole chicken = 3 cups cooked, de-boned, and diced meat.
4 pounds whole chicken = 4-1/2 cups cooked, de-boned, and diced meat.
5 pounds whole chicken = 6 cups cooked, de-boned, and diced meat.

Chili Powder

1 ounce = 5 Tablespoon
4 Tablespoons @ 3 Tablespoons paprika, 1 Tablespoon turmeric, 1/8 teaspoon cayenne, 1/8 teaspoon garlic powder
1 Tablespoon ! 1 teaspoon each oregano, cayenne, and salt

Chili Sauce

1 cup = 8 ounces
1 cup ! 9 ounces tomato sauce, 1/2 cup brown sugar, 2 Tablespoons vinegar

Chinese Five Spice Powder

1 ounce = 3 Tablespoons
@ equal parts ground cinnamon, cloves, fennel, anise, and pepper

Chives

1 ounce = 3 cups

Chocolate, Baking

See *Chocolate, semisweet* or *unsweetened*

Chocolate, Carob

See *Carob*

Chocolate Chips

12 ounces = 2 cups
12 ounces melted @ 1 cup cocoa, 1-1/2 cups sugar, 1/4 pound butter, melted, 1 Tablespoon paraffin.

Chocolate, Cocoa, Unsweetened

1 cup = 3 ounces
1 pound = 4 cups
1 ounce unsweetened chocolate @ 3 Tablespoons unsweetened cocoa, 1 Tablespoon butter or oil

Chocolate Crumbs

See *Crumbs*

Chocolate, German

1 square = 1 ounce
4 ounces @ 3 Tablespoons cocoa, 4-1/2 Tablespoons sugar, 2-3/4 Tablespoons shortening
@ semisweet chocolate

Chocolate, Grated

1 ounce = 4 Tablespoons

Chocolate, Mini-Chips

2 cups = 12 ounces

Chocolate, Semisweet

1 ounce = 1 square
1 ounce = 1/6 cup chocolate chips
1 ounce @ 3 Tablespoon cocoa, 1 Tablespoon butter, 3 Tablespoon sugar

Chocolate, Unsweetened Baking

1 square = 1 ounce
1 ounce = 4 Tablespoons grated
1 ounce @ 3 Tablespoons unsweetened cocoa, 1 Tablespoon butter
1 ounce > 3 Tablespoons unsweetened cocoa, 3 Tablespoons Butter Buds

Chutney

! equal parts apricot jam with dash cider vinegar
! equal parts orange marmalade with dash red pepper sauce

Cinnamon

1 ounce = 4-1/2 Tablespoons
1 teaspoon ! 1/2 teaspoon allspice, and pinch nutmeg

Citron

1 cup dried, sliced = 6-1/2 ounce

Cloves, Ground

1 ounce = 4 Tablespoons
1/4 teaspoon ! pinch each allspice, nutmeg, and black pepper

Coconut

1 pound = 6 cups shredded
3 ounces flaked = 1 cup

Coffee

1 pound grounds = 5 cups grounds
3 ounces = 1 cup grounds = 40 cups coffee
1/4 cup grounds = 10 cups coffee

Confectioners' Sugar

See *Sugar, powdered*

Coriander Seed

! equal parts crushed caraway seeds and ground cumin

Corn

4 ears = 4 cups kernels

Cornmeal

1 pound = 3 cups uncooked
1 pound = 12 cups cooked
1 cup uncooked = 5-1/2 ounces
1 cup uncooked = 4 cups cooked
! crushed corn chips, reduce salt in recipe

Cornstarch

1 ounce = 3 Tablespoons
1 cup = 5-1/8 ounces
1 pound = 3 cups
As a thickener: 1 Tablespoon thickens 1 cup liquid
1 Tablespoon @ 2 Tablespoons flour
1 Tablespoon @ 4 teaspoons arrowroot
1 Tablespoon ! 2 Tablespoons peanut butter

Corn Syrup

See *Syrups*

Cranberries

1 cup = 3 ounces uncooked
1 pound = 4 cups
1 pound makes about 3-1/2 cups sauce

Cream, Half-n-Half

1 cup = 8-1/2 ounces
1 cup @ 1/2 cup cream, 1/2 cup milk
1 cup @ 1/8 cup nonfat dry milk powder,1 cup water

Cream, Heavy

1 cup = 8-1/2 ounces
1 cup ! 1 cup whole milk, 1/3 cup nonfat dry milk powder,
1 Tablespoon oil
1 cup @ 7/8 cup milk, 3 Tablespoons butter
1 cup ! 2/3 cup skim milk, 1/3 cup oil
1 cup ! 1 cup milk, 3 Tablespoons butter

Cream, Light

1 cup = 8-1/2 ounces
1 cup ! 7/8 cup milk, 2 Tablespoons butter

Cream of Tartar

1 teaspoon = 1/8 ounce
1 ounce = 3 Tablespoons

Cream, Sour

1 cup = 8-1/2 ounces
1 cup ! 1 Tablespoon lemon juice, 2/3 cup nonfat dry milk powder, water to make 1 cup
1 cup ! 3 Tablespoons butter, 7/8 cup buttermilk or plain yogurt
1 cup @ 1 cup cottage cheese, blended on high until smooth, 1/4 cup buttermilk
1 cup @ 1/3 cup melted butter, 3/4 cup sour milk

Cream, Whipping

1 cup = 2-1/4 cups whipped
1 cup whipped = 1 cup frozen whipped topping

Crumbs

Use your blender or food processor in short bursts of power to finely crumble any of the following crumb materials. Expensive, pre-boxed options are just what they claim: crumbs! Why pay so much?

Crumbs, Bread

1 cup dry = 3 ounces = 4 slices bread
1 cup soft = 2 slices bread
1 cup soft @ 3/4 cup cracker crumbs
1 cup soft @ 1/2 cup dry bread crumbs

Crumbs, Cake

1 cup dry = 3 ounces

Crumbs, Chocolate Wafer

1 cup = 19 wafers = 3 ounces

Crumbs, Corn Flake

1 cup = 3 cups whole flakes = 3 ounces

Crumbs, Cracker
1 cup = 29 saltines = 3 ounces

Crumbs, Graham Cracker
1 cup = 13 crackers = 3 ounces

Crumbs, Vanilla Wafer
1 cup = 22 wafers = 3 ounces

Crushed Red Pepper Flakes
1 ounce = 5 Tablespoons

Cumin
1 ounce = 4 Tablespoons
! 1/3 anise and 2/3 caraway seeds, crushed

Curry Powder
1 ounce = 4 Tablespoons
! Turmeric

Dates
1 pound = 2-1/2 cups chopped
6 ounce whole pitted = 1 cup

Dill Seed
1 ounce = 1/3 cup
! fennel or anise
! equal parts caraway and celery seeds

Dill Weed
1 ounce = 1/2 cup
visual look-alike @ fennel
for cooking @ equal parts tarragon and parsley

Double-Acting Baking Powder
1 ounce = 2 Tablespoons
1 teaspoon @ 1-1/2 teaspoons single-acting baking powder

Dry Mustard
1 ounce = 5 Tablespoons
1 teaspoon @ 1 Tablespoon prepared mustard

Duxelles

@ You can pay a small fortune for duxelles (mushroom sauce) in the specialty section or you can make up your own for next to nothing on a rear burner while working on another kitchen project. Chop mushrooms to desired size and cook in butter over low heat, stirring occasionally, until reduced by half; store in refrigerator until needed. For richer flavor, add chopped onion and parsley while cooking.

Egg Beaters

1/4 cup @ 1 egg
See substitution options below.

Eggs

Jumbo:	4 = 1 cup whole	5 = 1 cup whites	11 = 1 cup yolks
Extra-large:	4 = 1 cup whole	6 = 1 cup whites	12 = 1 cup yolks
Large:	5 = 1 cup whole	7 = 1 cup whites	14 = 1 cup yolks
Medium:	5 = 1 cup whole	8 = 1 cup whites	16 = 1 cup yolks
Small:	6 = 1 cup whole	9 = 1 cup whites	18 = 1 cup yolks

Substitute 1 egg >! 1 heaping Tablespoon soy flour, 1 Tablespoon water
1 egg >@ 1/4 cup egg substitute
1 cup egg whites = 3 cups whipped

Eggnog

= Blend in blender: 6 eggs, 4 cups milk, 3/4 cup sugar, 1/2 teaspoon salt, 1/2 teaspoon vanilla, dash nutmeg
! vanilla ice cream and nutmeg

Evaporated Milk

See *Milk, evaporated*

Extracts

1 ounce = 2 Tablespoons

Fennel Seed

! anise seed

Figs, Dried

1 cup = 7 ounces
1 pound = 2 cups chopped

Fish Sauce

1 cup ! 3/4 cup soy sauce and 1/4 cup anchovy paste

Flour

See specific types or listings under *Thickeners*

Flour, Barley

1 cup = 4 ounces
Substitute for all-purpose flour 1 cup for 1 cup, up to a maximum of half the flour in the recipe

Flour, Bread

1 cup = 4 ounces
1 cup = 1 cup all purpose flour,
1 Tablespoon gluten flour ! equal parts all purpose flour

Flour, Buckwheat

1 cup = 3-3/4 ounces
Substitute for all-purpose flour 1 cup for 1 cup, up to a maximum of half the flour in the recipe.

Flour, Cake

1 cup = 4-1/4 ounces
1 pound = 4-1/2 cups
@ 7/8 cup all-purpose flour, 2 Tablespoons cornstarch for each cup of cake flour

Flour, Cottonseed

1 cup = 5 ounces
Substitute for all-purpose flour 1 cup for 1 cup, up to a maximum of half the flour in the recipe.

Flour, Gluten

1 cup = 3-1/2 ounces
Substitute for all-purpose flour 1 cup for 1 cup, up to a maximum of half the flour in the recipe.

Flour, Graham

1 pound = 4 cups finely milled
Substitute for all-purpose flour 1 cup for 1 cup, up to a maximum of half the flour in the recipe.

Flour, Pastry

1 cup = 4 ounces
Substitute 7/8 cup all-purpose flour per cup required.

Flour, Peanut

1 cup = 4 ounces
Substitute for all-purpose flour 1 cup for 1 cup, up to a maximum of
half the flour in the recipe.

Flour, Rice

1 cup = 4-1/2 ounces
Substitute for all-purpose flour 1 cup for 1 cup, up to a maximum of
half the flour in the recipe.

Flour, Self-Rising

1 cup = 5 ounces
1 cup @ 1 cup minus 2 teaspoons all purpose flour, 1-1/2 teaspoon baking powder and 1/2 teaspoon salt
8 cups @ 8 cups all-purpose flour, 5 Tablespoons baking powder, 2
Tablespoons sugar, 1 Tablespoon salt.

Flour, Unbleached White

1 ounce = 4 Tablespoons
1 cup = 4-3/4 ounces
1 pound = 3-3/4 cups unsifted
1 pound = 4 cups sifted

Flour, Whole Wheat

1 cup = 3-3/4 ounces
1 pound = 4 cups unsifted
Substitute for all-purpose flour 1 cup for 1 cup, up to a maximum of
half the flour in the recipe.

Frosting

1 pound = 3-1/2 cups
Recipes on page 153

Garlic, Clove

1 clove @ 1/8 teaspoon garlic powder
1 clove @ 1/8 teaspoon garlic salt
1 clove = 1 teaspoon minced garlic

Garlic, Crushed

1 teaspoon = 1/8 ounce
1 ounce = 3 Tablespoons

Garlic, Powder

1 teaspoon = 1/8 ounce
1 ounce = 3 Tablespoons

Garlic Salt

1 teaspoon = 1/8 ounce
1 ounce = 3 Tablespoons

Gelatin, Unflavored

1/4 ounce envelope = 2-1/2 teaspoons
2-1/2 teaspoons thickens 1 pint of liquid

German-Style Chocolate

See *Chocolate, German*

Ginger

1 Tablespoon chopped fresh = 1/8 teaspoon ground

Graham Crackers

1 pound = 40 squares
1 cup coarse crumbs = 9 squares
1 cup fine crumbs = 11 squares
! equal parts crushed ginger snaps
! equal parts crushed vanilla wafers

Granola

11 cups = 6 cups quick oats, 2 cups nuts/seeds,
1 cup coconut, 1 cup wheat germ, 1 cup brown sugar,
1/2 cup oil, 1/4 cup water, 1 Tablespoon cinnamon,
2 teaspoons vanilla, 1 teaspoon salt mixed and baked
spread out on cookie sheet at 350°F for 30 minutes.

Grated Fruit Peel

1 teaspoon fresh peels = 1/2 teaspoon dried
1 orange = 2 Tablespoons zest
1 lemon = 1-1/2 teaspoons zest

Green Onions

9 green onions with tops = 1 sliced onion
5 green onions with tops @ 1 cup chopped

Green Peppers

1 medium pepper = 6 ounces = 1 cup diced
1 medium pepper @ 4 Tablespoons dried green pepper flakes

Ground Beef

1 pound = 2-1/2 cups browned meat
@> turkey burger

Ham

1 pound = 2-1/2 cups ground
1 pound = 3 cups cubed
@ turkey ham

Hash Browns

4 ounces frozen = 3/4 cup

Herbs

1 Tablespoon fresh = 1 teaspoon dried
1 teaspoon dried = 1/4 teaspoon ground
See entries for specific types of herbs for further details.

Hollandaise Sauce

1 cup = 1/2 cup butter, 2 Tablespoons lemon juice and 1/8 teaspoon salt
heated in saucepan until gently boiling. Slowly add 3, well-whisked,
large egg yolks, one a time, beating constantly until thickened.
! equal parts white sauce (for hot recipes)
! equal parts mayo (for cold recipes)

Hoisen

1 cup @ 1/2 cup ketchup, 2 Tablespoons molasses,
1 Tablespoon soy sauce and 1 teaspoon Chinese five-spice powder

Honey

1 cup = 12 ounces
1 cup @ 1 cup corn syrup
1 cup @ 1-1/4 cup sugar, increase liquid in recipe by 1/4 cup
See also *Oil and sugar substitutes*

Horseradish

1 Tablespoon fresh grated @ 2 Tablespoons bottled
1 Tablespoon horseradish ! 1 teaspoon wasabi

Hot Pepper Sauce

1 teaspoon @ 1/4 teaspoon cayenne
1 teaspoon @ 1/2 teaspoon crushed red pepper flakes
! equal parts Tabasco

Italian Seasoning

1 ounce = 1/2 cup
! Basil
! Oregano

Jams/jellies

1 cup = 11 ounces

Ketchup

1 cup = 10 ounces
1 cup ! 9 ounces tomato sauce, 1/2 cup brown sugar, 2 Tablespoon vinegar (for cooking purposes only)

Kidney Beans

1 pound dry = 2-1/2 cups dry
1 pound dry = 6 cups cooked
1 pound can = 2 cups cooked
3/4 cup dry beans = 1 pound canned

Kitchen Bouquet

1 Tablespoon ! 1 teaspoon caramelized sugar

Lard

1 pound = 2 cups
@ shortening

Lemon

1 pound = 3 to 5 lemons
1 whole lemon = 3 Tablespoons juice, 1-1/2 teaspoon rind

Lemonade

1 cup @ 1 Tablespoon lemon juice, 1-1/2 teaspoon sugar, water, and ice to equal 1 cup

Lemon Juice

1 lemon = 2-3 Tablespoons lemon juice
1 ounce = 2 Tablespoons
1 teaspoon ! 3/4 teaspoon vinegar

Lemon Peel

1 medium lemon yields 2 Tablespoons rind
2 Tablespoons rind @ 1/2 cup lemon juice
2 teaspoons rind @ 1/2 teaspoon lemon extract

Lentils

1 pound = 2-1/2 cups = 5 cups cooked

Lettuce

1 pound = 6 cups bite-size pieces

Lima Beans

1 pound dry = 2-1/2 cups = 6 cups cooked

Lipton Onion Soup Mix

1 package = 3 Tablespoons
1 package @ 2 Tablespoons onion soup base (see *Bouillon*)
1 package @ 1 Tablespoon beef or onion bouillon, 2 Tablespoon onion flakes

Mace, Ground

1 ounce = 4 Tablespoons
! nutmeg
! cinnamon

Maltaise Sauce

1 cup = Melt 1/2 cup butter. Blend 3 eggs and 1 Tablespoon lemon juice on high until smooth. Pour egg mixture into saucepan. Heat at medium-high, stirring constantly, and adding a drizzle of butter as you stir, until all is smooth and barely bubbling.

Margarine

1 pound = 2 cups
1/2 cup = 8 Tablespoons = 1/4 pound
1/2 cup = 5 Tablespoons
1/4 cup = 4 Tablespoons
@ butter
! butter = flavored shortening (see can for details)
1 cup ! 7/8 cup oil (for cooking only)
1 Tablespoon !> fat-free Butter Buds (not suitable for frying)
1 Tablespoon !> 1 teaspoon butter-flavored powder, increase liquid in recipe by 1 Tablespoon
1 cup !> 7 Tablespoon buttermilk powder, water to equal 1 cup

Marjoram

1 ounce = 1/2 cup
@ thyme

Marmalade

1 cup = 11 ounces
! jelly

Marshmallows

1 cup = 13 large
10 ounces = 40 large
1 pound = 64 large = 4 cups
10 ounces = 4 cups mini-marshmallows
1 cup = 25 minis

Marshmallow Cream

7 ounce jar ! 10 ounce marshmallows melted with 4 Tablespoons butter

Mayonnaise

2 cups = In blender, combine 2 eggs, 1 Tablespoon lemon juice, 2 teaspoons sugar, 1 teaspoon dry mustard, 1/2 teaspoon salt, and 1/4 cup oil. Blend high until smooth, keep blending as you slowly drizzle in the remaining oil, until all oil is absorbed.
1 cup @> 1 cup Miracle Whip Free, 2 Tablespoons extra liquid

Meat, Ground Raw

1 pound = 2 cups raw = 1-1/2 cups cooked

Milk

1 cup = 8 ounces
@ 4 ounce evaporated milk, 4 ounces water
@ nonfat, skim, 1%, 2%, or whole
@ 1/3 cup nonfat dry milk powder, water to make 1 cup

Milk, Almond

1 cup @ 1 cup whole or soy milk

Milk, Buttermilk

1 cup @ 5 Tablespoons buttermilk powder, enough water to make 1 cup
1 cup ! 1 cup milk, 1 Tablespoon vinegar or
lemon juice: let stand 5 minutes
1 cup ! 1 cup milk, 1 teaspoon each baking soda, and baking powder
1 cup ! 1 cup yogurt

Milk, Evaporated

12 ounces = 1-1/2 cup
1 cup @ 1 cup light cream
1 cup @ 1 cup half-and-half
1 cup @ 2/3 cup dry milk granules, water to equal 1 cup
Reversed: 12 ounces evaporated milk, 12 ounces water = 3 cups milk

Milk, Evaporated Skim

12 ounces = 1-1/2 cup
1 cup @ 1/3 cup nonfat dry milk powder, water to equal 1 cup
Reversed: 12 ounces evaporated skim milk, 12 ounces water = 3 cups
skim milk

Milk, Nonfat Dry Milk Powder

1 cup reconstituted = 3-1/2 ounces powder = 1/3 cup powder, water to
equal 1 cup

Milk, Skim

1 cup = 8 ounces
1 cup @ 1/3 cup nonfat dry milk powder, water to equal 1 cup

Milk, Sour

1 cup = 1 Tablespoon vinegar, milk to equal 1 cup
1 cup ! 1 cup yogurt
1 cup ! 1 cup buttermilk

Milk, Soy

1 cup ! 1 cup whole or almond milk

Milk, Whole

1 cup = 8 ounces
1 cup @ 1/2 cup evaporated milk, 1/2 cup water
1 cup @ 1/3 cup nonfat dry milk powder, 2-1/2 teaspoons butter, 7/8 cup water
1 cup ! 1 cup buttermilk, 1/2 teaspoon baking soda
1 cup ! 1 cup soy or almond milk

Mint

1 Tablespoon fresh mint @ 1/8 teaspoon mint extract

Molasses

1 cup = 12 ounces
1 cup @ 3/4 cup sugar, 1 Tablespoon extra liquid

Monosodium Glutamate

1 ounce = 5 Tablespoons
@ Accent

Mushrooms

1 pound fresh = 12 ounces can
1 pound fresh = 3 ounces dried
20 whole = 5 cups sliced

Mushroom Steak Sauce

See *Duxelles*

Mustard

1 Tablespoon prepared @ 1 teaspoon dry
1 Tablespoon prepared = 1 teaspoon dry, 1 Tablespoon white vinegar
@ 1/2 quantity horseradish

Mustard Seed

1 Tablespoon @ 2 teaspoons dry mustard and
1 Tablespoon prepared mustard

Naan

@ equal parts pita bread
@ equal parts flour tortillas

Nacho Chips

1 ounce = 15 chips
1 pound = 15 cups whole
1 pound = 7 cups crushed

Napa Cabbage

@ equal parts Bok choy
! equal parts Swiss chard
! equal parts Savoy cabbage

Navy Beans

1 pound = 2 cups dry = 5 cups cooked

Neufchátel

@ cream cheese

Nonfat Dry Milk Powder

See *Milk, nonfat dry milk powder*

Noodles, Egg

1 pound = 7 cups cooked
7 ounces = 4 cups cooked

Noodles, Lasagna

1 pound = 12 to 24 noodles
12 noodles @ 1-9x13" or 2-loaf pan recipes of lasagna

Noodles, Macaroni

1 pound = 4-1/2 cups cooked
1 cup raw = 2 cups cooked

Noodles, Spaghetti

1 pound = 6 cups cooked

Nutmeg

1 ounce = 4 Tablespoons
! mace, cloves, or allspice

Nuts

1 pound in shell = 1 cup nutmeats
1 pound chopped = 3-3/4 cups
4 ounces nutmeats = 1 cup chopped
! rolled oats baked at 425°F until crunchy and golden

Nuts, Almonds

3-1/2 pounds in shell = 1 pound nutmeats
1 pound nutmeats = 3 cups
1 cup whole shelled = 4-1/2 ounces
1 cup slivered = 3-1/2 ounces
@ macadamia nuts

Nuts, Chestnuts

1-1/2 pounds in shell = 1 pound shelled = 2-1/2 nutmeats

Nuts, Hazelnuts

2-1/4 pounds in shell = 1 pound shelled = 3-1/2 cups nutmeats
@ macadamia nuts
@ almonds

Nuts, Pecans

2-1/2 pounds in shell = 2 cups shelled = 4-1/2 cups unshelled
@ walnuts
! hazelnuts

Nuts, Pistachios

1 pound in shell = 2 cups shelled = 3
! hazelnuts

Nuts, Walnuts

2 pounds in shells = 1 pound shelled
1 pound shelled = 4-1/2 cups halves
1 pound shelled = 3-3/4 cups pieces
@ pecans
! hazelnuts

Oatmeal

1 pound = 2 cups raw
1 pound = 8 cups cooked
1 cup raw = 1-3/4 cups cooked

Oats, Rolled

1 pound = 4-3/4 cups raw
1 cup = 3-3/4 ounces
1 cup @ 3/4 cup flour (in cooking/baking)

Oil

1 ounce = 2 Tablespoons
1 cup = 7 ounces
1 cup !> 2/3 cup nonfat dry milk powder, water to equal 1 cup
1 cup !> 7 Tablespoons buttermilk powder, water to equal 1 cup

Oil-and-Vinegar Dressing

@ 1 part vinegar to 2 parts olive oil
! 1 part lemon juice to 2 parts olive oil

Oil-and-Sugar Substitutes

Replace 1-1/4 cups sugar, 1/4 cup oil with 1 cup honey
Replace 1 cup sugar, 2 Tablespoons oil with 1 cup corn syrup

Olives

15 large pimento-stuffed = 1 cup sliced
36 medium = 1 cup sliced
48 small = 1 cup sliced

Onions

1 medium = 1/2 cup diced = 1/3 cup sautéed
1 medium @ 2 Tablespoons onion flakes
1 medium @ 2 teaspoons onion powder
1 medium @ 1 teaspoon onion salt and
reduce salt in recipe by 1/2 teaspoon

Onion Flakes

1 ounce = 4 Tablespoons

Onion Powder

1 ounce = 4 Tablespoons

Onion Salt

1 ounce = 3 Tablespoons

Onions, Green

9 green onions with tops = 1 cup sliced
@ equal parts onions

Onion Soup Mix

See *Lipton Onion Soup Mix*

Oranges

1 pound = 3 medium
1 medium = 7 Tablespoons juice, 2 Tablespoons rind
1 medium = 3/4 cup diced

Orange Peel

1 medium orange yields 3 Tablespoons rind
3 Tablespoons @ 1/2 cup orange juice (and reduce liquid in recipe)
2 teaspoons rind @ 1 teaspoon orange extract

Oregano

1 ounce = 1/2 cup
! quantity x 1.5 marjoram

Oreo Cookie Crumbs

1-1/4 pounds = 6 cups crushed

Oyster Sauce

! equal parts soy sauce and black bean sauce

Pan Coating Spray

5 ounce can = coating for about 60 – 9x13-inch pans
@ butter-coated paper towel

Paprika

1 ounce = 5 Tablespoons
1 teaspoon ! 1/2 teaspoon cayenne

Parsley

1 bunch = 1/2 cup chopped
! equal parts chervil

Parsley Flakes

1 ounce = 3 cups

Peaches

1 pound fresh = 4 medium
1 pound = 2 cups sliced
5-1/2 ounces dried = 1 cup

Peanut Butter

1 ounce = 2 Tablespoons
2 cups @ 1-1/2 cup salted peanuts
ground fine, 1/3 cup peanut oil and
honey to taste

Peanut Butter Chips

12 ounces = 2 cups

Peanuts

1 pound in shells = 3 cups in shells = 1-1/2 cups shelled

Pears

1 pound fresh = 4 medium
1 pound fresh = 2 cups sliced

Peas

1 pound dry = 2-1/2 cups raw = 6 cups cooked
15 ounce can = 1-1/2 cups peas
1 pound fresh = 3 cups

Pepper

1 ounce = 3 Tablespoons

Pepperoni

! equal parts hard salami

Peppers & Hot Sauces

1 Tablespoon fresh diced = 1 teaspoon dried
Use the following to determine a good substitution based on hotness levels:
Mild = Bell peppers, red, orange, purple, and yellow, pimiento; sweet banana and cherry peppers
Medium = Poblano and chili peppers
Hot = Jalapenos, Tabasco, and cayenne
Blazing = Habanero

Pimiento

2 Tablespoons chopped ! 3 Tablespoons chopped red pepper

Pineapple

8 ounce canned = 1 cup drained

Pistachios

1 pound in shells = 3 cups unshelled = 2 cups shelled

Plum Sauce

! equal parts mango chutney

Popcorn

2-1/2 pounds kernels = 10 cups kernels
1/2 cup kernels = 12 cups popped

Poppy Seed

1 ounce = 3 Tablespoons

Potatoes

1 pound = 3 to 4 medium raw
1 pound = 4 cups raw diced or sliced
1 pound = 2-1/4 cups cooked deiced or sliced
1 pound = 2 cups mashed

Potato Chips

1 pound = 15 cups
1 pound = 7 cups crushed
4 ounce bag = about 60 chips

Potato, Instant Flakes

1 pound = 16 cups flakes
1 cup flakes = 1-1/2 cups mashed potatoes

Potato Starch

@ equal parts cornstarch

Poultry Seasoning

1/2 cup = 2 Tablespoons marjoram, savory,
and sage, 1 Tablespoon thyme, 2
teaspoons rosemary.

Prunes

1 pound dried = 2-1/4 cups pitted
1 pound cooked and drained = 2 cups

Pudding Mixes

I have tried many recipes for dry pudding mix equivalents and have
found all to be disappointing in one way or another. When boxed mixes
go on sale, I stock up on the flavors we enjoy. If I happen to run out,
most recipe books offer numerous "from scratch" pudding recipes that
taste great, although all require cooking time.

Puff Pastry

! Phillo dough
! pie crust

Plum Sauce

2 cups = 16 ounce can of whole plums in heavy syrup,
1/3 cup apple cider vinegar, 2 Tablespoons sugar
and 4 teaspoons ground ginger heated through.

Pumpkin Pie Spice

1 ounce = 4 Tablespoons
1 cup @ 1/2 cup cinnamon, 1/4 cup ginger, 2 Tablespoons ground
cloves, 2 Tablespoons nutmeg

Queso

= Crockpot 2 hours on high 1 cup shredded Monterey
Jack, American and cheddar cheeses (3 cups total),
1 cup heavy cream, 12 ounce can RoTel tomatoes,
3 Tablespoons jalapeño peppers, and 2 Tablespoons
minced garlic.

Raisins

1 cup = 5-1/4 ounces
1 pound = 2-1/2 cups

Refried Beans

1 can = 16 ounces = 2 cups
= 2 cups cooked, mashed pinto beans, 3 Tablespoons vegetable oil, 1 Tablespoon chili powder, 1/2 teaspoon salt: fry over medium-low heat for about 5 minutes.
> 2 cups cooked, mashed pinto beans, 1/2 cup Butter Buds, 1 Tablespoon chili powder, 1 teaspoon salt: fry over medium-high heat for about 5 minutes. Watch carefully to prevent scorching.

Rhubarb

1 pound = 2 cups cooked

Rice, Instant

1 ounce = 1/3 cup dry = 2/3 cup cooked
1 cup raw = 2 cups cooked

Rice, White, Regular

1 pound = 2 cups dry = 6 cups cooked

Rice, Wild

1 ounce = 3 Tablespoons = 1/2 cup cooked
1 cup = 2 cups cooked
1 pound = 9 cups cooked

Rosemary

1 Tablespoon fresh = 1 teaspoon dried
rosemary, 1 teaspoon parsley flakes
! equal parts oregano
! equal parts basil

Roux

2 Tablespoons @ 1 Tablespoon flour, 1 Tablespoon melted butter
2 Tablespoons @ 1 Tablespoon cornstarch, 2 Tablespoons cold water

Saffron

1 teaspoon ! 1Tablespoon turmeric

Sage

1 Tablespoon fresh = 2 teaspoons rubbed
1 Tablespoon fresh ! 2 teaspoons ground

Salt

1 ounce = 4 teaspoons

Salted Crackers

1 pound = 160 squares
1 cup crumbs = 7 squares coarsely crumbled

Sausage

1 pound = 2 cups browned
@> turkey sausage
! ground beef, a few drops liquid smoke

Savory

! 1/2 thyme and 1/2 parsley

Scallions

See *Green onions*

Sesame Seeds

! very finely chopped almonds and a few drops sesame oil

Shallot

1/4 cup @ 1/4 cup chopped onion and 1 teaspoon minced garlic

Shortening

1 cup = 7 ounces
1 pound ! 1/2 pound butter, 1 cup oil whipped in blender (refrigerate)
1 pound ! 2-1/4 cups margarine (refrigerate)
1 cup ! 7/8 cup oil
1 cup !> 2/3 cup nonfat dry milk powder, water to equal 1 cup
1 cup !> 7 Tablespoons buttermilk powder, water to equal 1 cup
!> nonfat yogurt

Shrimp

1 pound small = 50 shrimp
1 pound jumbo = 20 shrimp

Shrimp Cocktail Sauce

Recipe on page 148

Shrimp Paste

! equal parts anchovy paste

Soup Bases

1 ounce = 4-1/2 teaspoons
@ 1 to 1-1/2 teaspoon, 1 cup water = 1 cup soup
See also *Bouillon*

Soy Sauce

1 ounce = 2 Tablespoons
1/4 cup @ 1 teaspoon caramelized sugar, 1 teaspoon beef bouillon, 3 Tablespoons water
1/4 cup @ 3 Tablespoons Worcestershire, 1 Tablespoon water

Spike

1 teaspoon = 1/8 ounce
1 ounce = 3 Tablespoons
@ seasoning salt

Stock

1 cup = 8 ounces
Many recipe books offer instructions for assembling rich stock bases including broth from freshly stewed meats and vegetables; when possible, this is ideal. When stock is needed immediately and no fresh broth is available, the following options work:
1 cup ! 2 teaspoons bouillon, 1 cup water
1 cup ! 1 Tablespoon soup base (see *Bouillon*), 1 cup water

Strawberries

1 quart fresh = 4 cups sliced
10 ounce frozen = 1 cup

Sugar

See also *Corn Syrup*, *Honey*, *Molasses*, and *Oil-and-sugar substitutes*.

Sugar, Brown

1 cup = 6 ounces
1 pound = 2-1/2 cups firmly packed
1 pound ! 2-1/4 cups white sugar
1/2 cup @ 1/2 cup granulated sugar, 1 Tablespoon molasses: whir in blender

Sugar, Granulated White

1 pound = 2 cups
1 cup ! 1-1/2 cups molasses, reduce liquid by 3 Tablespoons
1 cup ! 1 cup corn syrup, reduce other liquid by 1/4 cup
2 cups ! 1-1/2 maple syrup, reduce other liquid by 1/4 cup
1 cup ! 2/3 cup honey, 1/4 cup flour (or omit flour and reduce liquid by 1/4 cup)
1 cup ! 1 cup brown sugar
1 cup ! 2 cups powdered sugar

Sugar, Maple

1 cup = 6 ounces
1/2 cup @ 1 cup maple syrup, reduce other liquid by 2/3 cup

Sugar, Powdered

1 cup = 5 ounces
1 pound = 3 cups
4 cups @ 2-1/2 white sugar whirred in blender until fine

Sweetened Condensed Milk

1 can = Microwave 3 Tablespoons butter with
1/3 cup water until boiling. In blender, blend with
1/3 cup white sugar, 1 cup nonfat dry milk powder

Sweetened Condensed Milk, Fat Free

1 can >= Microwave 3/4 cup water until boiling.
In blender, blend with 3/4 cup white sugar and
1 cup, 2 Tablespoons nonfat dry milk powder

Syrup

1 cup = 12 ounces
Basic = 1 part water + 2 parts sugar, boiled until thick.
Flavored = Basic, 2 teaspoons flavoring
Corn Syrup: 1 cup @ 1 cup sugar, 2 Tablespoons liquid
Caramel, page 156
Chocolate, page 155
Crème de Menthe, page 50
Honeyed Fruit, page 141
Maple, page 164

Tabasco®

1 teaspoon = 1/6 ounce
1 ounce = 2 Tablespoons
Few drops of Tabasco @ dash of cayenne
4 drops of Tabasco @ 1/8 teaspoon cayenne

Tahini

1 ounce = 2 Tablespoons
= sesame seeds in food processor with enough sesame seed oil for
smooth paste
! equal parts almond butter

Tamari

1 ounce = 2 Tablespoons
! equal parts soy sauce

Tapioca

2 Tablespoons quick cooking = 4 Tablespoons pearls
1 Tablespoon @ 2 Tablespoons cornstarch and 2 Tablespoons cold water
as thickener
1 Tablespoon @ 1/4 cup flour and 2 Tablespoons cold water as thickener

Tarragon

1 Tablespoon fresh = 1 teaspoon dried
1 Tablespoon fresh @ 3/4 teaspoon crushed anise seed

Tarter Sauce

2 cups = 2 cups miracle whip or mayonnaise,
1 chopped onion (optional), 1/4 cup pickle relish,
dash garlic salt

Tea

1 pound = (yields) 125 cups

Thickeners

1 Tablespoon flour thickens 1 cup liquid
1 Tablespoon flour @ 1/2 Tablespoon cornstarch
1 Tablespoon flour @ 2 teaspoons arrowroot
1 Tablespoon flour @ 1 Tablespoon quick-cooking tapioca
1 Tablespoon flour @ 1/2 Tablespoon potato flour
1 Tablespoon flour ! 1 Tablespoon peanut butter
! add mashed potato flakes, a little at a time, stirring constantly until
desired consistency is achieved.

Thyme

1 ounce = 1/2 cup
! marjoram

Toffee

! caramels

Tomatoes

1 cup canned = 1-1/2 cups whole
1 pound canned whole = 3 medium
1 medium = 1 cup chopped
1 pound = 3 tomatoes
1/2 cup tomato sauce, 1/2 cup water @ 1 cup packed tomatoes, blended
1 cup canned @ 1-1/3 cups cut up fresh, simmered 10 minutes

Tomato Juice

1 cup = 8 ounces
1 cup ! 1/2 cup tomato sauce, 1/2 cup water

Tomato Paste

3/4 cup = 6 ounces
6 ounce can, 1 cup water = 15 ounces tomato sauce
1 Tablespoon ! 1 Tablespoon ketchup

Tomato Purée

1 cup = 8 ounces
1 pound 13 ounce can tomatoes @ 15 ounces tomato sauce, 1/2 cup
water
1 cup @ 2 Tablespoons paste, water to make 1 cup

Tomato Sauce

2 cups = 15 ounces
15 ounces = 3/4 cup tomato paste, 1 cup water
15 ounces = 2 pounds cooked, seasoned tomatoes

Tomato Soup

1 can = 10-3/4 ounces
1 can @ 1 cup tomato sauce, 1/4 cup milk

Tomato, Sundried

1 ounce = 10 tomatoes
1/2 cup @ 1-1/2 canned tomatoes, drained
1/2 cup ! 2 Tablespoons tomato paste
1/2 cup ! 4-6 plum tomatoes

Tortilla Chips

See *Nacho chips*

Turmeric

! saffron (brings same coloration without ruining taste)
! curry powder (closest flavor)

Turkey Breast

7 pounds cooked, de-boned breast = 12 cups meat, 3 cups broth
@ chicken breast

Turkey Burger

1 pound = 2-1/2 cups browned
@ ground beef

Turkey Ham

1 pound = 2-1/2 ground
1 pound = 3 cups cubed
@ ham

Turkey, Whole

1 pound = 6 ounces cooked, de-boned
6 ounces cooked = 1 cup
14 pounds cooked, de-boned = 14 cups meat, 7 cups broth
@ chicken

Unflavored Gelatin

1/4 ounce envelope = 2-1/2 teaspoons

Unsweetened Chocolate

1 square = 1 ounce
1 ounce @ 3 Tablespoons cocoa, 1 Tablespoon shortening
1 ounce @ 3 Tablespoons carob powder, 2 Tablespoons liquid, reduce
sugar in recipe by 1/4 cup

Unsweetened Cocoa

1 cup = 3 ounces
1 pound = 4 cups
1 ounce unsweetened chocolate @ 3 Tablespoons, 1 Tablespoon butter
or oil

Vanilla Extract

1 ounce = 2 Tablespoons
! almond extract

Vinegar

1 ounce = 2 Tablespoons
1 teaspoon ! 2 teaspoons lemon juice
Type substitutions:
Balsamic @ rice
Cider @ malt
Malt @ cider
Rice @ balsamic
White @ cider
Wine @ cider

Vinaigrette

= 3 parts oil to 1 part vinegar or lemon juice
! equal parts any salad dressing

Wasabi

1 teaspoon @ 2 teaspoons horseradish

Wheat Allergy Flour Alternative

1 cup = 1/2 cup cornstarch, 1/2 cup potato, rice, or rye flour, 2 teaspoon baking powder: sift all together 6 times.

Whipped Topping

3 ounces frozen = 2 cups
8 ounces @ 1 cup whipping cream, whipped and sweetened
See also *Cream, whipping*

Wines for Cooking

1/2 cup ! 1/4 cup vinegar, 1 Tablespoon sugar, 1/4 cup water (not for use in sauces)
1 cup ! 3 Tablespoons lemon juice, 1 Tablespoon sugar, and water to 1 cup
Marsala ! apple juice
Red ! beef, chicken broth or stock, tomato juice or red wine vinegar
Rum 1/4 cup @ 1 Tablespoon rum extract, water to 1/4 cup
Rum ! pineapple juice flavored with almond extract
Sherry ! orange or pineapple juice
White wine ! chicken broth or stock with dash white wine vinegar
White wine ! white grape juice with dash white wine vinegar

Worcestershire Sauce

1 ounce = 2 Tablespoons
1 Tablespoon @ 1 Tablespoon soy sauce, dash of Tabasco
! Steak sauce

Yeast

1 Tablespoon @ 1/4 ounce
1 cup = 4 ounces
1 package @ 2-1/2 teaspoons
3.5 ounce yeast cake @ 1 Tablespoon active dry yeast

Yogurt

1 cup = 8 ounces
1 cup ! 1 cup buttermilk
> 1 cup nonfat yogurt
! sour cream
! cottage cheese blended smooth

Appendix II

Handy Charts

Keeping cooking data assembled in one central location is a great way to save time. If you collect helpful cooking charts and information from newspapers and magazines, add a three-ring pocket folder to your Kitchen Notebook and tuck your favorites inside. Be sure to enter the chart titles in the index so you remember where you put them.

The Common Measurements Chart is a handy reference tool. Like the Up-and-Down Chart in Chapter 4, consider making a photocopy of it and taping it to the inside of a kitchen cupboard door for convenient access.

Common Measurements Chart				
1/8 Cup	=	2 tablespoons	=	6 teaspoons
1/4 cup	=	4 tablespoons	=	12 teaspoons
1/3 cup	=	5 tablespoons + 1 teaspoon	=	16 teaspoons
3/8 cup	=	1/4 cup + 2 tablespoons	=	18 teaspoons
1/2 cup	=	8 tablespoons	=	24 teaspoons
2/3 cup	=	10 tablespoons + 2 teaspoons	=	32 teaspoons
5/8 cup	=	1/2 cup + 2 tablespoons	=	10 tablespoons
3/4cup	=	1 2 tablespoons	=	36 teaspoons
7/8 cup	=	3/4 cup + 2 tablespoons	=	14 tablespoons
1 cup	=	16 tablespoons	=	48 teaspoons
2 cups	=	1 pint	=	32 tablespoons
4 cups	=	I quart	=	64 tablespoons

Unlike many baked foods, cakes and brownies require precise cooking times for success. Over- or undercooking a recipe by even, 10 minutes may result in unsatisfactory results. Whenever possible, follow a recipe's instructions for time, temperature, and pan size, but if you are rewriting a recipe for a different size pan, the chart on this page will help you determine the correct baking time. Always use the oven temperature given in the original recipe.

All cakes and bars may be baked in a preheated 325°F oven in glass pans or in a 350°F oven in all other types of pans. Unless otherwise noted, grease and flour your pans.

Average Baking Times for Various Pan Sizes (for Most Cakes and Brownies)		
Number of pans	**Pan size**	**Baking time**
1	8 by 8-inch	25-30 minutes
1	9 by 9-inch	30-35 minutes
1	9 by 13-inch	35-40 minutes
1	10-inch Bund	45-55 minutes
2	9-inch rounds	35-40 minutes
2	8-inch rounds	30-35 minutes
3	8-inch rounds	20-25 minutes
8	4-inch cupcakes	30-35 minutes
24	2-1/4 inch cupcakes	20-25 minutes

The Alternative Pan Size Chart will help you decide if your fancy mold
will work for a given recipe, and will provide alternatives if your 9 by
13-inch pan is already in use.

Alternative Pan Size Chart	
When the recipe calls for:	**You could use:**
4-cup baking dish	9-inch pie plate 8-inch round cake pan small loaf pan
6-cup baking dish	8- or 9-inch round cake pan 10-inch pie plate loaf pan
8-cup baking dish	8-inch square pan 11 by 7-inch casserole loaf pan
10-cup baking dish	9-inch square pan 11 by 7-inch casserole 15 by 10-inch jelly roll pan
12-cup baking dish	13 by 8-inch casserole (up to 12 cups) 13 by 9-inch casserole (up to 15 cups) 14 by 10-inch roasting pan (up to 19 cups)

Mold Volume Chart

Melon mold (7 by 5 by 4 inches) holds 6 cups
8-1/2 by 2-1/4 -inch ring mold (with open center) holds 4-1/2 cups
9-1/4 by 2-3/4 -inch ring mold (with open center) holds 8 cups

If you live at a high altitude you may already have a conversion chart posted in your kitchen. But just in case you don't, or if you are new to high-altitude cookery, this chart will help you provide great food every time.

High-Altitude Cooking Adjustments

For altitudes 2,500-4,000 feet

- Increase baking powder by 1/4 teaspoon for each teaspoon recommended.
- Decrease liquid by 1 to 2 tablespoons for each cup required.
- Decrease baking temperature 10 to 15 degrees.

For altitudes 4,000-6,000 feet

- Decrease sugar by 1/2 teaspoon per cup for each 1,000-foot elevation.
- Use 2 level teaspoons additional flour per cup recommended.
- Decrease baking powder, baking soda, or cream of tartar by 1/4 to 1/2 teaspoon, or use only three-quarters of the amount called for in the recipe.
- Increase liquid by 2 to 3 tablespoons per cup recommended.

For altitudes over 6,000 feet

- Decrease sugar by 1/4 cup for each cup required.
- Decrease baking powder by 1/4 teaspoon for each teaspoon required.
- Increase liquid by 3 tablespoons for each cup recommended.
- Increase baking temperature 10 to 15 degrees.

Timing Adjustment Chart for Microwaves.		
600-700 watt ovens use cooking times given in recipes:	**500-600 watt ovens add 15% to cooking time:**	**400-500 watt add 35% to cooking time:**
15 seconds	17 seconds	20 seconds
30 seconds	35 seconds	40 seconds
1 minute	1 minute 10 seconds	1minute 20 seconds
2 minutes	2 minutes 20 seconds	2 minutes 40 seconds
3 minutes	3 minutes 30 seconds	4 minutes
4 minutes	4 minutes 35 seconds	5 minutes 25 seconds
5 minutes	5 minutes 45 seconds	6 minutes 45 seconds
10 minutes	11minutes 30 seconds	13 minutes 30 seconds
15 minutes	17 minutes 15 seconds	20 minutes 15 seconds
20 minutes	23 minutes	27 minutes
25 minutes	28 minutes 45 seconds	33 minutes 45 seconds
30 minutes	34 minutes 30 seconds	40 minutes 30 seconds

Chicken Cutlery for Savings

1. Begin by removing any loose pieces from the inside of the bird. Rinse the chicken and then cut the wing portion from the body, rotating the wing as needed to help the separation.
2. Bend the leg joint back and cut through the meat and skin until the hip joint is free. Cut around the bone, not through it.
3. Cut toward the drumstick to separate it from the thigh.
4. Hold the body (neck end down) and remove the backbone by cutting down along each side of the bone and through the rib joints.
5. Cut a V through the white cartilage at the neck, exposing the dark bone at the center of the breast.
6. Remove the bone by bending the breasts back and forth. Cut the two breast meat pieces apart with a knife.

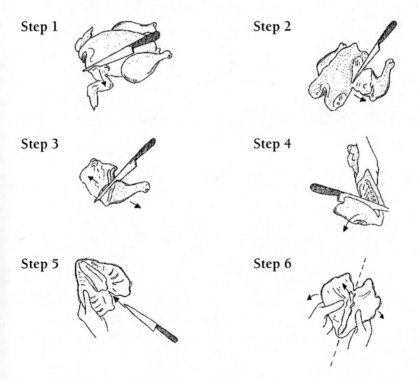

Step 1

Step 2

Step 3

Step 4

Step 5

Step 6

Index

After Words

Continue your friendship with Marnie at http://www.Marnie.com.

1. Request free "Marnie Minute" updates including links to online training.
2. Find out when Marnie is coming to a city near you.
3. Join Marnie's mentorship club to gain access to all of her online resources.

If this book has encouraged you, share it with others!

- Gift a copy to the home food managers on your birthday or Christmas list.
- Suggest it to moms, home economics- and adult education- instructors.
- Tuck it inside a congratulatory gift box for a hunter (or his wife).
- Start a cooking club using the strategies in this book to share meals with families in need.
- Ask your local bookstores and public libraries to carry copies.
- Write a book review or conduct an email interview with Marnie for your church newsletter, a local paper, favorite magazine or ezine.

Watch for more Marnie Method Books.

"Kitchen Shortcuts: Saving Time & Money in the Minutes You Have," is the third book in the Marnie Method Series for Super Busy Women. The first is, "Feeling Loved: Connecting with God in the Minutes You Have." The second is, "Minute Memoirs: Capturing What You Can in the Minutes You Have." Her strategies will reduce your stress and increase you enjoyment of life. Watch for series details and the next release at http://www.Marnie.com.

CPSIA information can be obtained at www.ICGtesting.com
225622LV00001B/1/P